IDAHO

Gratefully—
To: Bob Hebert
    From: Idaho Woodcarvers

        Oct. 12. 1985

IDAHO

PHOTOGRAPHY BY JOHN MARSHALL
TEXT BY CORT CONLEY

GRAPHIC ARTS CENTER PUBLISHING COMPANY
PORTLAND, OREGON

International Standard Book Number 0-912856-93-9
Library of Congress Catalog Card Number 85-71059
Copyright © 1985 by Graphic Arts Center Publishing Company
P.O. Box 10306 • Portland, Oregon 97210 (503) 226-2402
Editor-in-Chief • Douglas A. Pfeiffer
Designer • Robert Reynolds
Typographer • Paul O. Giesey/Adcrafters
Printer • Graphic Arts Center
Bindery • Lincoln & Allen
Printed in the United States of America

Frontispiece: Aspen, *Populus tremuloides,* interspersed with Douglas fir near Obsidian in the Sawtooth Valley, provides the brightest autumnal foliage in the West. Aspen are the most widespread of North American trees. Much larger than its eastern counterpart, the western variety's bark and buds provide food for moose, elk, deer, and grouse. Beaver regard the inner bark as their favorite food. Aspen wood is valueless for lumber, but it can be used for pulp.

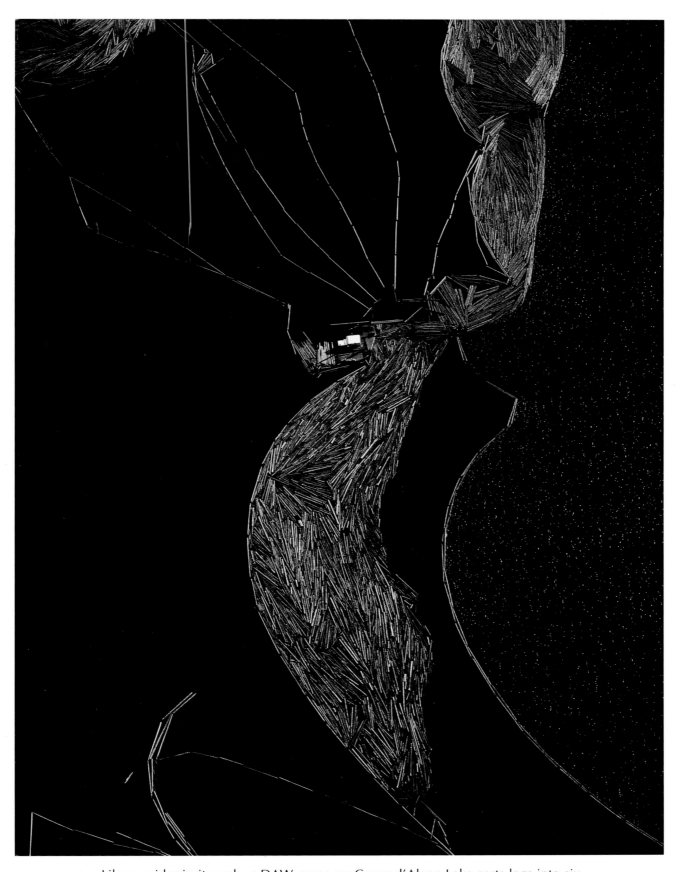

Like a spider in its web, a DAW crane on Coeur d'Alene Lake sorts logs into six pockets by species: cedar, red fir, hemlock, white pine, tamarack, ponderosa pine. Logs enter the water at St. Maries on the St. Joe River and are towed in small brails to the lake. After they are bundled into log booms, Lafferty tugs tow the booms, equivalent to one thousand loaded logging trucks, across the lake to the sorter in about thirty hours. In summer, sorted logs are towed four miles down Spokane River to the DAW mill; in winter, when gates on Post Falls Dam are open, logs travel aided by current to the mill.

Sunrise and moonset on Lost River peaks near Mahogany Creek on the upper Pahsimeroi River drainage. The Lost River Range is the highest in Idaho. Intersected by a few passes, most of the crest is over ten thousand feet, and, with the exception of one mountain, contains all the peaks in the state over twelve thousand feet. Running north from Arco to Challis, the range is composed of Paleozoic and Precambrian sedimentary rocks complexly folded and faulted in overlapping sheets about 150 million years ago.

E-DAH-HO

Idaho. Light on the Mountains. Light on the Selkirks and the Purcells. Light on the Seven Devils, the Sawtooths, and the Salmon River Mountains. Strange word, Idaho. Three short, flat syllables cadenced with an Indian inflection. An enchanting name. Although a persistent historian has exposed the word as concoction, legend has permitted it roots — if Indians never used the word, then white men did, grafting it to a topography that matched the given meaning: "light on the mountains." Light on the Gospels, the Pioneers, and the White Clouds. Light on the Lost River Range, the Lemhis, the Beaverheads, the Bitterroots. Light on the Owyhees, the Centennials, and the Tetons. Standing stump-firm, the myth quietly persists like the light and the mountains themselves.

If the name Idaho is mysterious to most persons, its geographic coordinates are more so — puzzling margins on their mental western map. Only a native can draw a credible offhand sketch of this state. Some see in its outline a hatchet balanced on its head with its blade hard against the flank of Wyoming; others say that it resembles a rocking chair with its runners planted on Utah's nothern border; a few kinetic imaginations even argue for a ski boot with its backstay along Oregon and Washington, tongue and toe stubbed against Montana and Wyoming, cuff untucked at Canada.

The genesis of this problem may lie in the fact that between 1848 and 1868 the contours of Idaho had all the stability of a cumulus cloud. When the area was discovered (and it was the last state to be discovered by white men), it was considered part of the Oregon Country. By 1853 the newly created Oregon Territory included southern Idaho, while Washington Territory took in northern Idaho. Six years later, Oregon became a state, and all of Idaho became an eastern extension of Washington. Then, when gold discoveries at Pierce caused an eastward shift in population, Washington's apprehensive legislature fostered a modified eastern boundary, a northerly extension of Oregon's.

In 1863 Congress accepted the line, and President Abraham Lincoln signed the law creating Idaho Territory. This new entity included all of Montana and most of Wyoming. A year later Montana Territory was cropped away, and in 1868 Wyoming was cut loose as well, leaving Idaho with the profile it carried through statehood in 1890—and the consequent problems that vex it to this day. Northwest historian Earl Pomeroy aptly described the territory as bringing "under one ungainly jurisdiction a miscellany of geographical leftovers that socially and economically still look about as much to Washington, Oregon, and Utah as to each other."

Idaho's protean boundaries account for other peculiar legacies: it has two time zones (Mountain and Pacific) and more shared borders than any other western state. Its seven degrees of latitude are exceeded in the continental United States only by California and Texas. Idaho measures 320 miles at its southern base, and fifty miles wide at its northern tip. Shouldered against the Continental Divide, landlocked Idaho has a surface more varied than that of any other state except Alaska and California.

With elevations from seven hundred to over twelve thousand feet, Idaho enfolds the deepest canyon in North America, counts hundreds of square miles of lakes and fifteen thousand miles of rivers, and embraces lava craters, sage plains, waterfalls, cedar forests, and sand dunes. It is all here on a pelagic scale and, in comparison to the rest of the country, as uncrowded as the high seas.

Sometime in the summer of 1984, Idaho's population forded the one million mark. It was a significant, and, to some, a lamentable milestone. In 1870 fewer than fifteen thousand persons were living in Idaho Territory. Because mineral discoveries came significantly later than those made farther west, miners and settlers were part of a unique reverse migration. Growth percentages were highest, however, between 1900 and 1910, when emigrants hoping to acquire land under the Carey and the Reclamation acts swelled the population to 150,000. Still, there was "more room than furnishings."

In the 1970s Idaho experienced its greatest overall census increase, and the composition of the population flowed from rural to urban. But Idahoans living an urban life do so in small towns. Only Boise has a population of 100,000; the next largest town is less than half its size. Rexburg, with a census of 12,000, manages to rank among the ten largest cities.

The consequent lack of congestion, the sense of "room enough and time," is one of the contentments of Idaho. Figures clarify the reason: only nine states have a smaller population; in only six are residents spread more thinly. With 83,557 square miles, Idaho ranks thirteenth in area among the states. It is about the size of Ohio and Pennsylvania combined, large enough that most residents tend to measure distance by time: it is as far from Boise to Idaho Falls as it is from Washington, D.C. to New York City.

NORTH IDAHO
Reflected Sky

A lake, John Muir observed, is landscape's most expressive feature. In the landscape of memory, north Idaho is lakescape, a few hundred square miles of it: lacquered blue in midsummer, with an occasional boat trolling through the sun's reflection; silver gray in mid winter, a shield of silence deployed against the lidded sky. The three largest lakes, Pend Oreille, Coeur d'Alene, and Priest, are an eighteen thousand-year-old endowment of the Great Ice Age. Together with their capillary rivers, they are the nexus of the Panhandle, and the story of their exploration and development is, like the bewilderment of currents, still in motion.

> *... And they let*
> *this lake maintain them, summers, as they would.*
> *Their cabin had an arm of the bay for porch.*
> *Now all the Rorschach lakes*
> *deny their shorelines in blizzards, but I come*
> *back, far down these evenings, faithful, to glean.*
>
> William Stafford
> "Priest Lake"

Early trappers and miners in the Panhandle would have been astonished to learn that the green gold rooted in the soil all around them would one day be worth more than all their pelts and placer gold. Timber-heavy shorelines along Idaho's northern lakes and rivers were the shoals of the world's most splendid softwood forest at the turn of the century. In the 1890s, having skinned the white pine forests of the Great Lakes states, timber barons sent their scouts west; when those scouts entered the virgin stands of northern Idaho, they must have felt like Schliemann finding the gold of Troy. Magnificent trees, six feet in girth and two hundred feet high, grew thicker than quills on a porcupine. River roads were there for transportation, and compliant settlers came to claim the stands under the Timber and Stone Act, to "prove up," then sell out to the company — an obvious subversion of the law.

Northern Idaho's present is inextricably linked to its logging past. "Rolling the round stuff" became the most important activity north of Boise. The boom got under way a half-dozen years before President Theodore Roosevelt, by executive order, withdrew most of the unappropriated federal timberlands from exploitation and named them national forests. Readily accessible trees were taken first, and the harvest was year-round. Less accessible timber was transported in chutes and flumes over difficult terrain to creeks and rivers, where "river pigs" piked it down to the lakes for sorting and branding in boomstick corrals. Logs, cabled in brails for tugboats, were then towed across the lake to railhead or sawmill.

After several decades, corporate loggers realized that their own growth was dependent on a cycle of reforestation now called "sustained yield." At present, Idaho ranks fifteenth nationally in acres of commercial forestland. Timber production in the state, with an increase of less than one percent a year, has been almost static for twenty-five years; during that time half the sawmills in the state have vanished. What caused this skid?

One, Canada has almost doubled its share of the United States market, at the expense of Idaho mills, and two, production of lumber and plywood has shifted to the South. Such improvements as may be possible in north Idaho will likely come about through better timber management, greater concentration on specialty wood products (rather than framing lumber), and continued investment in the paper market. '

Today, the lake country invites tourism. Coeur d'Alene, a town that has been the object of "holiday excursions" almost since its founding in 1887, is undergoing its greatest alteration since tourist steamboats (once a fleet of fifty) went the way of the stagecoach. Between 1890 and 1910 weekend crowds of twenty-five hundred arrived on trains from as far away as Walla Walla to board the paddlewheelers and dine and dance their way across the lake, up the cottonwood-belted St. Joe, and back.

Summer tourists have continued to arrive as dependably as the lake's osprey, and in the 1980s promoters began to change the scale of the city's shoreline. In response, a shoreline-protection initiative was written to limit building heights to thirty feet, but not before a variance allowed construction to begin on a twenty-one-story hotel/convention center, including a marina, costing $40 million. Some have cheered the new growth because it represents local investment, local employment, and year-round visitor spending. Others, irked and disquieted, find the scope of the development an affront to the balance of the shorescape which attracted the visitors in the first place.

Just forty-five miles north of Coeur d'Alene is Sandpoint, a much smaller town that lounges on the shore of Lake Pend Oreille. Equally favored with pleasant views and pleasant streetscapes, it relies on summer tourists and winter ski traffic to Schweitzer Basin. Prevalent here, as well, are the tensions caused by social alteration and inroads upon tradition.

Even Priest Lake, the most northerly and loveliest lake of them all, with its lapis moire and its blue islands like basking whales, has been confronted with a vision of South Lake Tahoe. Again, the issues are complicated and easy answers are unavailable.

This country blanketed with sky colors is no longer a land of blue solitudes, undiscovered. Like other parts of the state, north Idaho's lakeland is facing a period of complex decisions and trade-offs among owners, users, and uses.

Lead Valley, Silver Lining

Last week everything went bad. The mine
collapsed like a tired lung,
the old miner's dreadful daughter
fled to Nevada in what remained
of his Chevy pick-up and his shoebox
savings account, taking the Randall boy,
half-Indian, with her, and the dog.

Ron McFarland
"Kellogg," 1983

Stream course dictates the contours of the historic Harris Creek Toll Road, twenty-five miles west of Idaho City. In 1872 the Boise County Commission granted Felix Harris rights to maintain the principal access route from the west to the Boise Basin mines. After crossing the Snake, traffic from Oregon traveled east up the Payette River to the toll road entrance, just southeast of Horseshoe Bend. Harris charged one dollar for a team and wagon. In 1907 the county purchased the gate for a public road; it is now used by logging trucks.

9

Built between 1905 and 1912, Idaho's capitol imitates the neo-classical pattern of the national capitol. Sandstone quarried from Table Rock at the north edge of Boise was laid over a steel framework. Corinthian columns were erected to support the dome, 208 feet above the rotunda floor. Italian craftsmen, brought to the city, made the columns of scagliola — a mixture of marble dust, gypsum, and glue. Between 1919 and 1921, the east and west wings were added for the House and Senate, which brought the cost of the building to $2 million.

Although Nevada calls itself the Silver State, Idaho has long been the nation's largest producer of silver. Driving east on Interstate 90 from Coeur d'Alene Lake into the west end of Silver Valley, one enters a twenty-mile circle, centered on Wallace, which ranks among the top ten mining districts in the world. Like several other valleys in this country, it has made poor men rich and rich men richer. Since 1884 the mines have disgorged metals, primarily lead, silver, and zinc, valued at $4.5 billion. They have yielded a billion ounces of silver, nearly half of it since 1940. Each year, for three-quarters of a century, this silver circle has produced from one-sixth to one-fourth of the nation's lead and silver.

It is an inexorable fact that mining, like a fire, consumes itself. The first mine to produce in the valley, the Tiger, went out like a blown match in 1908; in 1925 the famous Hercules closed; and in the fall of 1981, after almost one hundred years of continuous operation, Bunker Hill's directors announced that it was shutting down. With it went the largest payroll in north Idaho—over two thousand miners were left without work, and their loss affected an equal number of other jobs. A year later, another lead-zinc mine, Hecla's Star-Morning, active since 1889, pulled its machinery out and let the shaft flood. In 1981, Day Mines, Inc., established in the 1890s, was acquired by Hecla. Shortly thereafter, Hecla announced that it was moving its headquarters from Wallace to Coeur d'Alene. Residents of the valley, accustomed to fluctuations, had more than their share in those few years.

The tale of prospector Noah Kellogg's discovery of the Bunker Hill lode, when his recalcitrant jackass nodded toward it, is as well known in north Idaho as a hit tune. Unlike nearby placer mines, however, development of the Bunker Hill mine and the rest of the Coeur d'Alene lode was dependent on two factors: a transportation system and large amounts of capital. Both arrived with alacrity.

Capital was the more complicated matter. Corporate fortunes were needed to pump western wealth into eastern treasuries, and the list of millionaires whose money developed the mines and smelters in this valley reads like a *Who's Who* of nineteenth-century American capitalism: Jay Gould, J. P. Morgan, Simeon Gannett Reed, John D. Rockefeller, Cyrus McCormick, and the Guggenheim brothers.

Along with the robber barons came a twelve-year period of labor strife. Before it was over, there were strikes, blacklists, shootings and deaths, paid informants, a hijacked train, dynamited mills, martial law, federal troops, over a thousand arrests, a mining union crippled, and, later, a governor murdered. This valley is no stranger to violence or sudden change of fortune.

Hardrock mining is a rough and risky business. Early miners were troubled by silicosis, emphysema, and lead poisoning caused by the drilling dust from Revett quartzite. In 1972 the Sunshine mine became the focus of a national vigil, when fire broke out and trapped scores of men underground. Though heroic efforts finally allowed crews to reach the lower levels of the mine, they found only two survivors.

Nor is smelting ores without hazards. While much of the timber on the slopes of the valley between Pinehurst and Kellogg was taken for stopes and chutes and for fueling steam boilers, reforestation was impossible because of the sulfur oxides released by lead and zinc smelters for sixty years.

When the Bunker Hill smelters closed in the fall of 1981, the company remained in the news because of lawsuits filed by the parents of children who had allegedly suffered brain damage caused by lead emissions from the company's stacks. At present, the Environmental Protection Agency and the state, with money from the EPA Superfund, are working on a program to remove heavy metals from the Bunker Hill smelter and the surrounding thirty square miles.

Not all of the valley has shut down, however. In the past five years, silver production, especially for electronic and photographic purposes, has increased dramatically. The Lucky Friday, a mine that sold in 1936 for $120 in back taxes, has completed a new shaft to 6,200 feet, which makes it the nation's largest silver producer. In 1984, Hecla, Lucky Friday's owner, acquired Ranchers Exploration and Development Company and its large silver holdings for $200 million. The Sunshine mine, closed in 1982, reopened a year later and has completed a deeper shaft and a $20 million silver refinery. Bunker Hill has opened the Crescent silver mine and is using one circuit of the old mill for concentrating. Callahan Mining Company has committed $25 million to the Calladay Project, a mile-deep exploratory shaft. Moreover, four of the five largest silver mines in the United States are still located in the valley, and 50 to 60 percent of the nation's new silver is still produced here.

It may be axiomatic that mining is liquidation, but as one historian of the area, John Fahey, observed: "There is always the chance that an exhausted mine will spring to life with a hidden vein at depth, perhaps discovered by new techniques, and almost a certainty that in the cycle of minerals prices, nearly worthless ore of one decade will sell in the next."

Golden Solum

*Looking out through the wide elevator doors
into miles of hot, wavering
northwest Idaho wheat fields,
saturated and near boredom,
each of us expects the other to break the silence.
I begin.
"John. Describe these wheat fields.*

Gentle, hilly, not flat.
How would you do it?"
Oceans of sunlight wash over in the long space
before he speaks.
"It's hard. Everyone thinks of Kansas."

Robert Sund
"Bunch Grass"

Grasshopper plagues in Kansas in the 1880s drove farmers westward to take up early homesteads on the Palouse. Treeless, fenceless, combed and shorn, the new country must have made them feel at home; when they discovered that the hilltops and sidehills could be farmed as well as the bottomlands, they took to the area like honeysuckle to fencing.

Rolling in gentle undulations south from Coeur d'Alene Lake, the hills eddy around the city of Moscow and flood the countryside with a moat of color: chocolate furrows, glittery-ribbed in spring and fall; chive-colored sprouts that follow the first rains of winter; the soft, fluorescent green wheat of spring; rape fields, fire-yellow in May; and then, at last, in August and September, the lion-colored, lustrous dunes of wheat and barley.

As with any agricultural legerdemain, the colors of the crops reflect a meeting of earth and sky—and human proficiency. Remarkable silty loam soil has made this two thousand square miles the richest soft white winter wheat area in the world. ("Soft white" refers to the kernel, which is low in its percentage of protein and high in starch.)

All virgin soil is the aftermath of rock, climate, organisms, topography, and time working together at different rates. Loess, the parent body of the Palouse soil, often reaches a depth of one hundred feet, and its topsoil of eight to eighteen inches is blessed with high fertility, ready absorption, and abundant retention of moisture. Tracing the source of this unusual mantle is something of a geological puzzle, though one theory ascribes it to wind-blown silt from the Big Bend of the Columbia River, trapped by the moist grasslands of the Palouse over a period of twenty-five thousand years.

Since it is a region of non-irrigated farming, the Palouse depends upon the twenty inches of rain that fall between October and April. Relatively sheltered from the tempers of weather, it is an area dowered with seasonal rhythms so regular that a crop failure has never been known. Most of the Palouse is on a three-year rotation of crops: winter wheat, barley, and Alaska peas or lentils. Winter wheat is planted in the fall to ensure early germination and growth; barley, like peas, is planted in the spring.

Moscow, located in the middle of the Palouse, is Idaho's ninth-largest city; it was named by an unofficial postmaster, a homesteader born near Moscow, Pennsylvania. In 1888 the city became the seat of the only county in the nation established by an Act of Congress.

If the act was evidence of regional rivalry with nearby Lewiston, selection of Moscow in 1889 as the site for the University of Idaho, the state's land-grant college, was proof of sectionalism. Moscow was given the nod by the territorial legislature when the city agreed not to support a bid by the rest of north Idaho to join Washington in statehood. Now a focal point for the community, the University has nine colleges, a graduate school, and a law school and is the only comprehensive institution of higher learning in the state. It is entrusted with primary responsibility for research, instruction, and public service in the fields of agriculture, forestry, engineering, and mining. Located in an unparalleled agricultural district, in an essentially agrarian state, the school understandably has a distinguished record of contributions to Idaho farming and ranching.

Mechanization of American agriculture is a well-known story. In the Palouse, however, the tale has a few uncommon twists. Early farmers used the Schandoney hitch to handle teams pulling plows, harrows, and seed drills across the swollen hills. Larger teams, hitched to combines, consisted of sixteen to forty-four horses, and visitors from other farming regions were incredulous when they witnessed the feats performed with extended teams on the prairie. Between 1900 and 1930 there were more skilled teamsters to be found in the Palouse than anywhere else in the world.

In the 1930s, even as Will Rogers was saying, "The horse raises what the farmer eats, and eats what the farmer raises, and you can't plow in the ground and get gasoline," the Caterpillar tractor had begun to consistently outperform and displace the horse. More recently, articulated tractors with four-wheel drive showed such advantages in power and speed that most farmers by the mid-1970s were converted, and they now trace the contours of their land while comfortably enclosed in a cab, seated at hydraulic controls.

Technology and research may have been the salvation of American agriculture, but problems linked to the application of inorganic fertilizers and to tillage with modern equipment have begun to appear in the Palouse. Ammonium-based fertilizers have made the region's soils more acidic, and the solum, or farmable soil layer, has undergone a significant change. Further, erosion is greater in the Palouse than anywhere else in America because farmers pulverize the soil in a manner that horses did not, and rain carries off the silt— two-tenths of an inch yearly for each acre. That might seem niggling in so rich an area, but the solum is thin enough that in less than sixty years areas already eroded may be down to subsoil.

The success of crop scientists working at the University of Idaho and Washington State University, eight

Restless foliage prompted the name for quaking aspen. Father Pierre DeSmet, early missionary in Idaho, relates that the voyageurs had a superstition that this tree furnished the wood of the Cross and since then has always quaked. Leaves of the aspen are hinged on stems flattened contrary to the plane of the leaf, thus causing the famous flicker of light and shadow. This grove near Fairfield is only a short distance from Mays Creek and the state's record quaking aspen: 7½ feet in circumference and 86 feet in height.

Sown in the spring for harvest in the fall, two-row barley (called so for the position of the seeds) ripens with graceful awns on Camas Prairie near Grangeville. Growing conditions determine barley quality: if it meets high standards of carbohydrate in the seed it is sold for malt. Less selective feed barley brings a lower price. Idaho ranks, depending on the year, first or second among all states in barley production.

miles away, has disguised the problem. Semi-dwarf strains and disease-resistant varieties of wheat have pushed yields to one hundred bushels an acre against a national average of twenty. But as university agronomists explain, "There is no assurance that technology, whose curve has leveled, will continue to offset erosion-induced losses." Consequently, new methods and new tools have appeared. "No till," or plowless farming, and residue management are now Palouse vernacular. Increasingly, farmers are seeding through the stubble of previous crops. Chisel plows, "soil savers," which till deeper while leaving mulch on the surface to slow erosion, have replaced moldboards on some farms. Heavy, double-disk seed drills apply starter fertilizer with the seed and minimize soil disturbance. "No till," however, brings problems of its own, not the least of which are costs of new equipment and decreased yields. Perhaps minimum till will prove a better answer.

Society favors soil conservation, yet implementation of that policy in the Palouse inevitably comes solely out of the farmer's pocket. A wry Mexican proverb runs, "It is not the same to talk of bulls, as to be in the bullring." The farmer is in the ring every day—with weather, government regulations, interest rates, unpredictable markets, rising costs. His crop has all the surety of a lottery ticket.

But Palouse farm families have tenacious rootholds. Most have either operated the same farm all of their lives or, if they are younger, have grown up in one of the local communities and are now taking over a hand-me-down farm. For them, two generations are not all that far down the road. Traditions, technology, conservation, and public policy will have to work as complements to maintain the Palouse. The alternative is to squander in fifty years a foot and a half of soil that was eight thousand years in the hoarding.

Lewiston: Promise of the Sea

The Countrey about the forks is an open Plain
on either Side. I can observe at a distance on
the lower Lar. Side a high ridge of Thinly
timbered Countrey the water of the South fork
is a greenish blue, the north as clear as cristial.

Captain William Clark
Confluence of Snake and
Clearwater, 1805

On August 8, 1975, at 2:30 P.M., the new towboat *Idaho,* with Captain Mike Murphy at the wheel, easily maneuvered a large maroon barge loaded with 100,000 bushels of wheat into the current, bulled across the confluence where the Snake and Clearwater make their peace, and headed downriver to Portland, 375 miles away. Murphy's voyage represented the opening of a latter-day Northwest Passage, a welcome alternative avenue for the agricultural and timber industries, and the completion of a twenty-year project costing $900 million. Slackwater navigation had arrived at Lewiston, 730 feet above sea level, and the most eastern of West Coast ports.

In Idaho, Lewiston is a vintage town — the first to incorporate, and only a few months shy of having been the first permanent settlement in the Territory. Populated in 1861 as a result of a gold strike in the Clearwater Mountains about seventy-five miles to the east, Lewiston owed its location to the limits of river navigation. Since steamboats found it the only practical riverport in the region, the flat ground at the mouth of the Clearwater became the supply yard for the mines. Probably half the population during the first years were non-mining gold diggers, entrepreneurs of every description providing subsidiary, but essential, services. At the time, the land was still part of the Nez Perce Reservation, but in 1863 most of the Indians were whipsawed into a new treaty and the site was ceded to the United States.

President Lincoln signed the Organic Act establishing Idaho during the Civil War. He regarded territorial patronage as a means of maintaining loyal governments in the West. As a result Idaho was bedeviled with the worst collection of carpetbag governors in territorial history. Their escapades, which sank to the level of vaudeville, underscore the north-south rivalry produced by geographical isolation before rails, roads, and wires spliced the state, and explain much of the estrangement that lingers between the two sections to this day.

North Idaho factionalists were united in their demand to join with eastern Washington and western Montana in a new state. When borders solidified, sentiment in north Idaho coalesced around annexation by Washington, and in 1887 feelings were weighty enough to send a bill through Congress and onto President Grover Cleveland's desk. He exercised a pocket veto, however, in deference to an objection by his appointed Idaho governor. Statehood in 1890 settled the question, at least superficially, but it has been almost impossible for north Idaho to elect a governor or a United States senator, and the issue has come up in at least four elections since 1907.

Modern Lewiston is now knotted to the deepwater ports of Vancouver, Portland, and Astoria, and it feels the draw of the long rope of the Columbia: barges push wheat and barley west by the hundred thousand tons, churn seaward with lentils and peas, paper and tissue compacted in twenty-foot containers.

The city has renewed perspectives. Graced with numerous examples of frontier architecture, Lewiston's Main Street has undergone a remarkable renovation—facades have been restored, brick buildings sandblasted, a plaza cleared, and ample funds spent on landscaping. The local improvement district developed a plan with downtown businessmen, and early results encouraged reluctant merchants. Even Hotel Lewis and Clark, a landmark at First and Main, was admirably remodeled into office space by a local firm. Bill Hall, editorialist for the *Lewiston Tribune*, explains the rejuvenation: "These are pretty young towns in the West; they take about sixty or seventy years to rot, ten years for anyone to realize it, and another ten or twenty years to correct it."

Completion of the Port has influenced the city's revival. The docks are a terminal for rail and truck lines, the focus of exports and imports, a transportation hinge vital to farmers of the area, and a conduit for the paper products of Potlatch Corporation, the city's major employer. Seaport status has given Lewiston a more regional outlook and image.

In connection with the Port's overall plan, the Army Corps of Engineers has designed an extensive recreation system that winds eleven miles through three parks along the Snake and Clearwater levees. Here at the verge of the city, walkers, joggers, and bicyclists pursue their purposes as the river pursues the sea. Lower Granite Dam brought slackwater to the confluence of the Snake and the Clearwater; it also gave Lewiston a sense of the possible, a current and a course.

The Grander Canyon

Far down in distance a stream uncoils
Like nothing more than a glittering wire
Tangled in stone-slots, lost on the plain,
In distance dissolved, or down canyon gone.

Robert Penn Warren
"Mountain Mystery"

Sixty miles south of Lewiston lies Hells Canyon, a cleavage between Idaho and Oregon that accommodates the Snake River, and a sight which has never evoked indifference. Even its name, used as early as 1895, is indicative: "Hells Canyon, where the river winds like a serpent, and the rocks tower to such a height that they almost shut out the sun." Hyperbole, of course, but "austere," "gloomy," "somber" have cropped up in accounts by explorers ever since Wilson Price Hunt of the Pacific Fur Company led his expedition into the ragged chasm in 1812 and shied out as though he had stepped on a snake.

While the creation of Hells Canyon was something of an accident, its preservation was not. Two hundred and fifty million years ago, the region was part of a shallow inland sea, superseded over time by immense Lake Idaho. Eventually, continental tectonics rucked and pleated the Seven Devils through mile-deep layers of lava in the midst of the lake. Geologists hypothesize that a million years ago a south-cutting stream cleft the northern lip of the lake near Oxbow, and rapid erosion cut the present Snake River drainage, now deeper, measured in an angular fashion, than the Grand Canyon of the Colorado. Unlike the Colorado, however, steep creek mouths and abruptly incised side canyons are testaments to a young, vigorous river.

Archaeological work in the canyon, begun in the 1950s, suggests a chronology with four cultural phases, which extend from 4,500 B.C. until well into the last century. Artifacts and other remains tell us that the natives took big game, particularly deer; grinding slabs imply that seeds and roots were more important than fish. As tokens of their presence, these winter dwellers left circular "house pits" and vermilion pictographs along the benches above the river.

In the 1860s mineral strikes began to occur in the Seven Devils, where an irregular belt of copper deposits is embedded. Isolated mines like the Peacock, Blue Jacket, and White Monument began to ship ore by pack trains, until Albert Klienschmidt came to the Devils and built a freight road from the canyon rim to the river that is used by tourists to this day. He also contracted for a 165-foot steamboat to haul ore upriver to an Oregon railhead, but after two trips the price of copper plummeted and the vessel *Norma* was left like a turtle when the tank goes dry. She was ordered downriver by her owners. In 1895 Captain William Gray, the best steamboat pilot on the Columbia, arrived with his crew, caught the spring rise, and brought her through with scarcely a miscue. No steamboat accomplished the passage again.

Because its heavy stands of bunch grass became attractive only after more accessible range had either disappeared or been depleted, settlement by stockmen and ranchers came relatively late to Hells Canyon. With their arrival, river traffic took more utilitarian, if less colorful, forms.

The *Flyer* was, in 1910, the first boat on the Snake with a gasoline engine. She was thirty-six feet long and gimped upriver with sheepshearers and freight for ranchers. As business grew, competition surfaced and larger, more dependable craft were launched. River boats became the lifeline for families shoehorned into homesteads at the mouths of creeks where there was scarcely enough soil to bury a dog. Mail, groceries, wool, machinery—all were hauled on the river road. Even now, a mail boat makes once-a-week deliveries to a few folks who cling to the canyon lifeway.

In 1925 a young man, Amos Burg, came drifting through the canyon in a canoe rigged with oarlocks. He had embarked on his river journey in Yellowstone National Park three months earlier, and his arrival was the wellspring of recreational boating, the main business of Hells Canyon in the 1970s and 1980s.

Like speckled fish, cottonwood and alder leaves repose in a pool alongside Smith Creek, which drains Abandon Mountain in the northern Selkirks. Unlike black cottonwood, *Populus trichocarpa*, which can prosper along streams that run only a few weeks a year, alder, *Alnus tenuifolia*, must have its roots in water. Black cottonwood, which is the largest poplar in the world, grows at elevations of up to ten thousand feet, often with trunks three to four feet in diameter. Its dark leaves, silvery white beneath, shimmer in any summer breeze.

A Ray Holes saddle is as western as a pair of Charlie Dunn boots. Holes, a young leather worker, repaired his first saddle in 1933, then spent three years traveling through the Rocky Mountains and Canada learning the saddlemaker's art from old-time craftsmen. By the time he returned to Grangeville in 1936, he was ready to make saddles with three attributes: beauty, durability, and comfort. When Holes retired in 1973, his son took the reins and now employs his own children as well. The Holes family made this custom saddle, which sold for over ten thousand dollars, in honor of their shop's fiftieth anniversary.

After the Second World War, calculations of the river's hydropower potential and the canyon's capacities as a reservoir overshadowed all other considerations for almost two decades. Private power companies recognized the opportunity to profit from an abundant resource. Other, wider considerations held little candlepower at the time. Between 1955 and 1968 three Idaho Power Company dams corked one hundred miles of the canyon. But values change.

After a twenty-year struggle between proponents and opponents of six more dams, the United States Congress in 1975 established the Hells Canyon National Recreation Area. President Gerald Ford signed the bill designating sixty-seven miles of the Snake as part of the National Wild and Scenic Rivers system and classifying as wilderness 194,000 acres in two units divided by the river. A Forest Service team then worked for five years to develop a comprehensive management plan intended to maintain a balance among environmental concerns, recreational uses, and the stability of the local economy. Canyon slopes are now largely given over to a few packers and numerous hikers. Mountain sheep and goats have been reintroduced on the Seven Devils side, and, surprisingly, a grizzly bear was sighted in the high country in 1978. The river remains an avenue of commerce and recreation: in summer, raft-trip outfitters and weekend river runners with power boats; in season, hunters and fishermen; and year long, the Snake still sings its "fathoming music."

River Signatures

We give in to the persuasions of the river, floating
Swiftly downstream as well as the leaves beside us,
Ahead of us, with little choice
Which way it may be next
That we find ourselves
One boat-length farther along, taking the rough with
the smooth...

David Wagoner
"Downstream"

Webbed with fifteen thousand miles of river, more of them classified as "Wild and Scenic" than in any other state, Idaho lives among its rivers as with a trust. Historic rivers like the Kootenai, Lemhi, and Lochsa; workhorse rivers like the Snake and the Bear; fisherman rivers like Henrys Fork and the Clearwater; "tubing" rivers like the Boise and the Portneuf; rafting rivers like the Middle Fork and the Selway. To imagine Idaho without rivers is to imagine literature without poetry.

Whether viewed from an earth satellite or from Horse Heaven, the state's topography reveals an astonishing riverine gravure. Together, five of these incised scrawls carry an annual flow of 72 million acre-feet. Since rivers flow with the slant of the land and Idaho is wholly west of the Continental Divide, all this dampness (except for the Bear River) ends up in the Columbia River Basin.

River-supply shops sprinkle the state. Kayaks and rafts, driftboats and jet boats are car-topped and trailered summer and fall. Three-score outfitters advertise day trips and week trips; several hundred river guides are licensed yearly. All summer long, any reach of river deeper than a horse trough reveals a party fighting or following the persuasions of the current. In only twenty years their numbers have grown into the thousands, their value into the millions. How did it happen?

Perhaps answers can be found on the Salmon River, whose history and uses are representative. Known as the "River of No Return," its headwaters lie in the lap of the Sawtooths and flow four hundred miles to the Snake, fifty miles south of Lewiston. The course of the Salmon can be followed by highway for one hundred and seventy miles from the Sawtooth Valley to North Fork, then by paved and gravel road west another forty-four miles until the river recedes into the unroaded River of No Return Wilderness.

Members of the Lewis and Clark Expedition were the first white men to see the Salmon. After scouting west of what is now North Fork in the summer of 1805, they elected to press on by land over Lost Trail Pass. Captain William Clark had reconnoitered downstream with difficulty:

The River from the place I left my party to this creek is almost one continued rapid...the passage ...with Canoes is entirely impossible, as the water is Confined between huge Rocks & the Current beeting from one against another for Some distance below &c. &c...."

Between 1832, when two members of a Hudson's Bay trapping expedition drowned, and the 1890s, only three trips on the River of No Return are recorded. Most exotic was the third, whose conclusion at Salmon City in the spring of 1887 was witnessed by Robert Bell, a state mining inspector:

There arrived at that port...a boat shaped like a Chinese junk with dragon figurehead and tail. It had been towed and poled up the Salmon River from its mouth with a crew of ten Chinamen. This flat-bottomed boat was thirty feet long, had a six-foot beam, and carried all the tools, supplies and possessions of the crew, which had placer mined along the richer bars that border the river, over a year's period, and banked a large sum of gold on their arrival.

River traffic, then as now, was stimulated by the prospect of profit. Hardrock mines were discovered in the 1880s on the river at Shoup, about forty miles northwest of Salmon. Pack strings brought machinery and supplies by trail, until novice boatmen built scows with sweeps to see if they could haul bigger loads at less expense. A period of trial and mistrial smoothed out the difficulties, and by the 1890s tons of freight were being floated to the mines.

Sweepboats, roughly thirty feet in length, were handled with a pair of long poles, one at each end of the boat, fitted with blades that rested in the water. Pinned at a pivot point, these sweeps exerted enough leverage that the boatmen could stand on a deck above the cargo and, with deftly timed strokes, use the momentum of the current to maneuver their barge downstream. Once its freight was delivered, the scow was pried apart, the lumber sold, and the boatmen began their overland journey home—hence the name "River of No Return."

Captain Harry Guleke was the sweepboat pilot who became the informal "King of the Salmon," dominating local river traffic between 1896 and 1930. Strong as an axle tree, handsome and kindly, Guleke brought fame to the river, and, inadvertently, to himself. His expertise became legendary; magazine articles generated national recognition and added scenic, hunting, and movie-making trips to his schedule, which often stretched over ten months of the year. By 1912 Cap Guleke had hauled nearly three million pounds of freight; by 1925 he had over four hundred trips to his credit. Said Boise's *Idaho Statesman:* "He knows the rapids, the rocks, and the fitful wiles of the river as a preacher knows his Bible."

Non-freighting trips began on the Salmon at least as early as 1911, and in 1929 a party made the thirteen-day trip from Shoup to Riggins in rubber boats simply as a "sporting adventure." Trips with decked, wooden rowboats made in the 1930s gave further evidence of a trend. When World War II ended, inflatable rafts made of durable neoprene became available in surplus stores at reasonable prices, and before long boatmen were offering their services as guides on western waters. As techniques and equipment improved, Idaho, with its mesh of inviting rivers, established a reputation as the preeminent whitewater state.

A state board was appointed in 1961 to set standards for outfitters and guides. Permits, licenses, and user fees were established, and federal agencies developed management plans for the rivers within their jurisdictions and carefully divided use between professional and amateur river runners. Annual lotteries are now held for trip permits, and campsites are often assigned. Regulations have removed some of the spontaneity from river trips; but they are necessary limitations protecting the river from its admirers.

In 1980, as a result of the Central Idaho Wilderness Act, the seventy-nine-mile reach of the Salmon River from Corn Creek to Long Tom Bar was classified as "Wild." Since the River had survived federal plans for channel clearance, log drives, roads, and dams, the designation seemed well deserved and overdue.

SOUTH IDAHO

Desert Encounter

No one has ever said he goes "out" into the city,
We always say we go out into the desert.
It is out; out of self, out of presences.
Absence is what we have here.
In deserts we stand under something
That is not there, a sea, a mountain.

Radcliffe Squires
"Storm in the Desert"

Change comes on the crawl in Owyhee County. Take its name, for instance: it is the original spelling for Hawaii used by Captain Cook. Hawaiian trappers were employed in 1818 by Donald McKenzie in the Boise Basin; three of them explored the region southwest of Boise that winter, and when they failed to return in the spring their name was given to the desert and the mountains. While missionaries altered the spelling for the islands, the change never filtered this far east.

The Owyhees are a big country, almost one thousand square miles larger than the combined islands of its namesake, and the second-largest county in the state. In 1866 the area had a population of five thousand—miners and a few ranchers; in 1980 the population was eight thousand—ranchers and a few miners.

Miners in 1865 were busy at Silver City, fifty miles southwest of Boise. Every week, eighty-two mill stamps pummeled gold and silver worth an average of $70,000 from ore fed down the slopes. Now inaccessible in winter, a tourist magnet in summer with its forty weathered buildings, "Silver" is the queen of Idaho's ghost towns. In 1972 the entire ten thousand-acre site was placed on the National Register of Historic Places as a Historic District.

Today, only twelve miles away, one hundred and fifty miners work at the DeLamar silver mine next to a townsite whose mines produced $23 million in gold and silver between 1890 and 1914. The new operation, begun in 1977, uses a cyanide-system mill with leaching vats. Its open pit is one of the top ten silver mines in the nation, as well as one of the more cost efficient. Reserves are expected to last for twenty years.

Early ranchers were lured to the Owyhees by the mining-camp markets. Bands of sheep were driven from California; Texas Longhorns trailed north on a journey that required five months. According to an Idaho history published in 1884, "Cattlemen ... drove cattle here in large numbers, until today there are probably more in Owyhee County than in any other part of the territory. The summer range for cattle is almost inexhaustible, every hillside a luxuriant growth of bunch grass." Native grasses grew high as a saddle skirt, but as others heard of the plenteous range, which was free for all, it became overstocked.

On May 2, 1972, fire broke out in the 3,700-foot level of Silver Valley's Sunshine mine. About half of the day shift was successfully evacuated, the other half was the object of an intense eleven-day rescue effort directed by the U.S. Bureau of Mines. With ninety-one victims, it was the largest hardrock mining disaster in the nation in over fifty years. Ken Lonn's spartan sculpture of a miner thrusting his pneumatic drill skyward was dedicated on the second anniversary of the tragedy.

A cluster of scabland penstemon appears to have stemmed this two thousand-year-old flow of pahoehoe lava at Craters of the Moon. Seventy miles from Sun Valley, Idaho's only National Monument was established in 1924 by President Calvin Coolidge and contains at least thirty-nine separate lava flows. Once used as a geological instruction site for Apollo astronauts, much of the eighty-three-square-mile monument was designated a wilderness area in 1965. Apparently barren, the area supports a remarkable diversity of plants, birds, and mammals.

By the time the Owyhee Cattlemen's Association (the first in the state) was formed in 1878, estimates placed the number of cattle on the desert at 100,000 head. Then the weather went awry: the winters of 1887, 1888, and 1889 arrived on hard hooves, and when they drifted away there was not enough beef left on the plateau to hold a barbecue there. While ranchers turned their efforts to stockpiling winter hay, homesteaders elbowed in around creeks and waterholes once dominated by cattle kings, fenced their claims and, finding the Owyhee too arid for dryland farming and too inaccessible for irrigation, also turned to livestock ranching.

During the same decade, sheepmen used the opportunity to gain a tailhold on land once held exclusively for cattle, and by the turn of the century at least 150,000 wethers were scattered throughout the region. The lines between sheepmen and cattlemen were gradually drawn by mutual agreement and they were generally respected, but when migratory sheep outfits muscled through the same country, trouble inevitably flared.

Grass, the foundation of the livestock business, is a renewable resource. Light grazing, up to 40 percent of the plant, has little effect on the roots, but if more than half of the volume of the grass is grazed, growth is halted. By the late 1920s the range was overgrazed. As the writer H. L. Davis succinctly explained: "It got eaten up and destroyed, not by the introduction of sheep, as legend commonly makes out, but by the prevalence in the cattle-raising industry of hogs. Two-legged ones, who, judging that somebody else would get the grass if they didn't, hustled in every class of stock they could lay their hands on to eat it clean, ending up with sheep to burrow down and eat out the roots. Then they pulled out, firmly believing that the Lord's hand was set against them, and the country had a chance to recuperate."

Recuperation came in the form of the 1934 Taylor Grazing Act, supported by conservationists and the livestock industry. To curb heavy, injurious use of the public domain, the Grazing Service, forerunner of the Bureau of Land Management, issued grazing permits. Applicants were favored who controlled property capable of feeding livestock during the winter and who had used it together with federal range during the five years preceding passage of the Act. Land policy acts in 1976 and 1978 reinforced the improved conditions.

Despite reconditioning of the range, Idaho's sheep have ebbed from 2.4 million head in the 1930s to less than 350,000—the greatest decline in a hundred years. Causes are readily found. Since lamb is the only red meat for which the United States has no import quota, New Zealand has cornered the domestic market, and wool-growing, which in the 1890s was more important than mutton, has lost its significance with the rise of synthetic fabrics. With improved political conditions in Spain, Basque sheepherders from the Spanish Pyrenees no longer have reason to immigrate West, and replacements are harder to find. (Successful stockraisers in the Owyhees, the Basques of southern Idaho once constituted the largest colony outside their homeland.) Currently, herders come from Mexico, Chile, and Peru. They still trail bands with the seasons from Birds of Prey Refuge on the Snake River to McCall and from Rupert to Soda Springs, but these drives are merely vestiges of a useful, colorful business, again eclipsed by cattle ranching.

Cattle production has grown along with Idaho's agriculture, in part because cattle are fed barley and byproducts from potato and sugar-beet factories. For over ten years Idaho has had just under 2 million cattle and calves worth $500 million in annual gross income. But grazing range cattle on the Owyhee plateau is not like raising feedlot cattle. It's a scanty business. Each animal needs twenty or thirty acres of forage a month to hold its own, and the saying goes, "Out there, if she's gonna get any feed at all, a cow's gotta have a mouth three feet wide and travel thirty miles an hour." Having taken more turns than a tumbleweed, the cattle business is still here, and acceptance of some changes, howsoever begrudgingly, may explain why.

Perhaps the most difficult change was brought about by a federal court order that required the Bureau of Land Management to write an environmental impact statement for each of its districts. Emphasis shifted to competing interests and spawned the "Sagebrush Rebellion," but widespread public opposition to the disposal of public lands, and a change in administrations, quashed the issue. Gradually, the concept of accommodating a fair balance of other uses, and even of restricting uses when necessary to protect public lands, has won general acceptance.

Other changes have also proved irresistible. Crested wheat grass from Russia, in some cases superior to the original forage, has been introduced to the range. On hay ranches, pivot irrigation systems rhythmically water two hundred acres at a pass. Semi-trucks haul cattle from winter quarters to summer range and back again, saving pounds and forage. Researchers have developed vaccines, artificial insemination, pregnancy tests, growth implants. Computers measure range production and set guidelines for use related to temperatures and rainfall. Genetic engineering has begun to improve both livestock and plant species.

Yet large reaches of the Owyhee country are beyond all change. Some areas are so inaccessible that preliminary mapping by the United States Army did not begin until the 1950s, and the U.S. Geological Survey did not arrive until 1962. Much of the Owyhee is still a land of tall sage and runty juniper; of deer, antelope, coyotes, bobcats, bighorns, and mustangs; of fitful rivers and gumbo roads, and nameless gorges layered deep with lava flows.

Boise: Fort to Capital, Full Tilt

Boise is the richest city of its size in the United States, but Boiseans are not caste conscious. The well-being is evenly spread and the people don't care a hang how much dough you've got or who your old man was.
Bierne Lay
Saturday Evening Post
1946

When Major Pinckney Lugenbeel selected the wide apron below Table Rock for his new fort, he had bypassed an entire rock garden of poorer choices. The site lay near the convergence of the Oregon Trail and the roads between the Boise Basin and Owyhee mines. Cottonwoods crowded the banks of "La Riviere Boissee" (the "wooded" river) named by French trappers, and ample sandstone suitable for building rimmed the slope. On the Fourth of July, Lugenbeel's infantrymen, with the aid of a sawmill and quarry, began construction. They built well: one of the sandstone houses dating from the 1860s is considered the oldest occupied residence in the city.

News of Lugenbeel's choice traveled through the valley like a jackrabbit running from a sage fire. Seven men met with Tom Davis in his cabin on the Boise River and laid out a townsite between his homestead and the fort. They set the main street parallel to the river for three-quarters of a mile and donated choice lots in the five blocks on each side to prospective businesses in order to attract more settlers. Since the population of the new territory had shifted south with the gold discoveries in Boise Basin and the Owyhees in 1862 and 1863, the capital was also deftly transferred south from Lewiston within a year.

Boise Valley was garden, barn, and root cellar for the miners to the north and south: patchwork farms mottled eighty thousand acres around the capital in the 1880s. New York investors, aware that the railroad's projected arrival would provide a lucrative outlet for crops, financed a major irrigation canal from the Boise River across the valley—an endeavor so expensive that it was satisfactorily completed only when the Reclamation Service became involved in 1905.

As the valley's population grew, so did the need for water. Anderson Ranch Dam on the South Fork of the Boise and Lucky Peak Dam on the main river, both built with federal funds and completed in the early 1950s, provided a secure source of water for valley farms in the event of drought, and some protection from flooding as well. A fact little known even to residents of the region is that the valley supports the largest vegetable seed industry in the nation, in part because it is isolated

from disease and pests. Most of the vegetable seed in the United States—sweet corn, lettuce, radish, onions, beans—is grown here.

As Boise expanded in the 1960s, planning became the answer to the unruly growth that threatened valuable agricultural tracts. With expansion, Boise was firmly established as the dominant metropolitan area in the state. Sustained by its agricultural production and by light industry, the city also became a wholesale and retail distribution center and, just as important, the national headquarters for a number of major corporations: Boise Cascade, a Fortune 500 company producing lumber and paper; J. R. Simplot Company, a potato and fertilizer conglomerate; Ore-Ida Foods, the country's largest diversified frozen-food company; Albertson's, the nation's ninth-largest grocery chain; Trus Joist, a structural wood engineering firm; and Morrison-Knudsen Company, a large engineering and construction firm. Nowhere in the Intermountain West, not even in Denver, does one find so much indigenous corporate control. Reasons for the growth of capital include Idaho's low corporate income tax, absence of an inventory tax, minimum union representation, and high labor productivity.

Because it is the state capital, Boise is also a center for state and federal agencies. Government employment contributes balance to the local economy, while increasing numbers of professional workers augment Boise's urbanity. The city has been home for two chairmen of the Senate Foreign Relations Committee, William Borah and Frank Church, and for Secretary of the Interior Cecil Andrus. Cultural assets include the Morrison Center for the Performing Arts, the Boise Philharmonic Orchestra, the Boise Gallery of Art, the Idaho Historical Museum, and Boise State University.

In 1965 the Boise Redevelopment Agency, created under an urban renewal law, began efforts to revitalize forty acres of the city's core. Accomplishments with both public and private funds include a new city hall in 1977 and county administration building in 1980, partial restoration of the landmark Idanha Hotel, preservation of the Ada Theater, and construction of Idaho's tallest building, Idaho First Plaza. Nevertheless, for tangled reasons the marrow of the city has been neglected, despite the efforts of several developers. In 1984 a new developer was chosen to complete the renovation of the neglected eight-block area in the city's core, and residents look forward to an appealing mix of offices, stores, and open space.

Life in the City of Trees is enhanced by the amiable river that strolls through the middle of the city like an invited guest. Like the mountains and plains close by, the Boise River symbolizes the near-neighborhood of the wild. Boise's citizens use and appreciate their river, their parks, and their nearby national forests. Sewage-

The name for the Soldier Mountains above Fairfield is a legacy of the Bannock War of 1878. Shoshone and Bannocks from Fort Hall, starving because of governmental indifference to promises of annuities and food under the Treaty of Fort Bridger, left their reservation. A three-month skirmish ended with the deaths of Buffalo Horn and Chief Egan. Whitebark pines, limbs on the windward side, endure their own adversity at nine thousand feet. Some require four hundred years to grow three feet; cones take two years to ripen.

Beneath the raker of El Capitan Peak (9,901 feet) in the Sawtooths, just below Alice Lake. Exposures of glaciated batholithic granites make this thirty-mile-long range among the more spectacular in the country. National park status was first proposed for the Sawtooth Range in 1916, when Addison Smith and William Borah introduced bills in Congress. The idea was opposed by Gooding sheepmen because "it would close the gates to hundreds of thousands of livestock." In 1960, Senator Frank Church again introduced a bill, but it was 1972 before the area was set aside as a National Recreation Area.

disposal facilities constructed in the 1960s restored the river's clarity; now it is floated all summer long, and the trout taken from it are safe to eat. Under Idaho's comprehensive outdoor recreation program, a greenbelt project to connect all of Boise's river-area parks for several miles is well advanced. Funded in part by the Interior Department, the greenbelt is an essential element in the lives of Boise residents, and they share it: *Castor canadensis,* the beaver sought by the French trappers in 1833, is sufficiently active along the river that many trees have been protectively screened—both an inheritance, like others, that has survived.

Peaks Four Ways

Rainbows and cutthroats easy in the pool,
Elk in the bottomland in the winter, the mountains
Pearl white at dawn, then long blue shadows
Falling in the hot springs ...

Gary Holthaus
"Circling Back"

Idaho is mountains: welted with eighty-one named ranges and more than one hundred and fifty peaks, many still nameless, above ten thousand feet. While these mountains—rock-strewn slopes, scalloped ridges, hazy crags—stretch the length of the state, the most spectacularly convoluted area is underpinned by the Idaho batholith. A mosaic of geological units, the batholith, which means deep stone, extends three hundred miles north and south and seventy-five miles east and west. In central Idaho its eroded, granitic exposures display the most enheartening and indescribable geology in the state: the Sawtooths, White Clouds, Bighorn Crags, Salmons, and Bitterroots. Cardiograms. Views worth contemplating a whole week. These metamorphic storms rise through fathoms of air, aglow with abundant light.

Through some startling default, Idaho is the only state in the Rocky Mountains that has no national parks, but is has something rarer: wilderness, in the neighborhood of 9 million acres, untracked as the remotest region of any park. Designated wildernesss in Idaho includes 3.8 million acres; another 6.5 million acres of wilderness is unprotected. Opinions about how much of this land should be left unaltered vary. Some think that the main thoroughfares through these ranges should remain game trails, others, that they should be roads. Specifically, it is a tourney between timber, mining, and livestock associations, and citizen-preservationists. Regardless of contentions, some figures are useful.

Idaho ranks third among states with federally managed land. Holding 68 percent of the timberland in the state, the Forest Service provides 48 percent of the timber industry's requirements. For eleven straight years, Idaho has tied among the western states for the greatest financial loss on national forest timber sales.

The forest-products industry needs a reasonable assurance concerning its supply in order to make decisions on capital investments. But the president of a large Boise corporation entirely dependent on timber points out that "existing roadless areas [in Idaho] are not, and never have been economical to log." Average yields on commercial timberlands in Idaho are so low that the cost of building roads exceeds the stump-value of the timber.

Exploitation of mineral deposits in the region, however, is more feasible. In 1983 Standard Oil of Indiana began production at a strip mine on the east side of the River of No Return Wilderness that will produce 20 percent of the world's molybdenum. Golden Reef Joint Venture and Coeur d'Alene Mines are both involved with open pit mines on patented ground on the boundary of the wilderness area, and Asarco has an interest in molybdenum deposits in the White Cloud Peaks.

Parochial and catholic views are at issue, as well. Idaho's senior senator, in a burst of chauvinism one can understand, if not justify, declared, "I guess it's fair to say those of us who live in Idaho resent a little bit having somebody come in from Akron, Ohio, and tell us how we ought to live. It's our land and our people are affected by it. We cannot afford to exist simply as a playground for the rich who live somewhere else." Others, however, feel that the issue of wilderness is a national one; that the lands are held in trust for all Americans, and especially for Idahoans fortunate enough to live in proximity to them.

One side argues that the value of wilderness must be determined by the price its convertible resources will bring on the market today. The difficulty on the other side is that recreation is a utility, not a tangible product, and its value can only be determined if its users can add in the value of their time.

Ample evidence indicates that Idahoans value wilderness. Tourism is touted as the third-largest industry in the state, and recent research by the Idaho Travel Council shows 63 percent of Idaho travelers list the state's scenic beauty as their major motive for vacationing here. Surveys by the Forest Service in north and central Idaho reveal residents account for 40 to 90 percent of backcountry use, with the most popular activities camping, fishing, boating, hiking, hunting, and horseback riding.

Idaho wilderness, whether designated or not, provides habitat for fish and shelters substantial populations of big game: elk, deer, black bear, cougar, bighorn sheep, and goats, smaller numbers of moose, and remnant populations of grizzly bear, mountain caribou, and wolves. A list of 366 wildlife species occurring in the River of No Return Wilderness indicates the wealth of this biological reservoir. In 1983 the

Fish and Game Department issued Idaho residents 75,000 hunting licenses, 120,000 fishing licenses, and 152,000 combination licenses. Five years ago, a U.S. Fish and Wildlife Service survey estimated that one-half of all households in Idaho have a hunter and three-fourths have a fisherman. In this light, the Idaho wilderness does not appear to be a reserve for rich easterners.

Nearly 200,000 non-residents, however, buy licenses to hunt or fish in Idaho each year, and the state's thirteen hundred outfitters and guides provide services for those visitors who lack the skill, equipment, and local knowledge for a wilderness experience. This business brings the state an estimated $35 million each year.

Setting aside lands under a recreative umbrella may or may not violate conventional benefit-cost criteria, but such lands, like minerals and unlike forests, are not reproducible resources. The benefits are already consonant with the lives of most Idahoans. Demand for wilderness use in Idaho, according to a Forest Service analysis, will increase 30 percent by the year 2000 and 120 percent over a fifty-year period. Nor is wilderness a new kind of public land reservation. As zoologist and educator Aldo Leopold pointed out twenty years ago, "it is only a new kind of dedication within our public forests . . . it is not land and life in a museum cabinet to be viewed only from the outside. It is rather an asset to be enjoyed by many forms of use that leave no legacy of alteration . . ." Surely it is no accident that Idaho, with its limited population and almost limitless vantages produced well-known outdoor writers like Jack O'Connor, Ted Trueblood, Elmer Keith, Will Ormond, and Clare Conley.

The Aorta

Hills lean away from the loss of this river
while it draws on lakes that hang still among clouds
for its variable journey among scars and lava,
exiled for that time from all green for days
and seeking along sandbars of bereavement at night.

William Stafford
"By the Snake River"

Grand Teton National Park ranger Joe Shellenberger and his friend were intrigued by the inconsistencies on maps showing the source of the Snake River. One map placed the source on the boundary of Teton National Forest; another showed it farther north, inside Yellowstone Park. Curious, they decided to go see for themselves. For three fall days, they hardscrabbled up a canyon between Lynx and Falcon creeks into the wilderness of Two Ocean Plateau. Following the ever-diminishing thread, they finally arrived at a large spring flowing in rivulets from a twenty-foot fissure at the base of the canyon wall. A check of the canyon above showed it was dry. Elated, they clambered back

down to the spring and drank from its frosty waters. It was October, 1970, and the source of America's sixth-largest river was identified at last.

The Snake is a thousand-mile river draining 100,000 square miles and its waters tangle with forty tributaries in six states. From Wyoming it flows southwest in a graceful crescent across the plains of southern Idaho before angling north to Lewiston and a hundred miles beyond, joining the Columbia.

Called the "Nile of Idaho," it is the spinal cord of the state. Without the Snake, southern Idaho would resemble Nevada. More than half of the state's population lives within fifty miles of the river; six of the nine largest towns depend on its irrigated corridor for their economy. In turn, most of the state's manufacturing industries—factories processing potatoes, beet-sugar refineries, milk processors—rely on products of Snake River irrigation.

Since the Snake River Valley receives only nine to twelve inches of rain a year, and no surface water augments the Snake for 160 miles along its northern margin, where does the flow come from? Most of it originates in the snowpack of the more humid Rocky Mountains to the north and east; but part of it is derived from the Big and Little Lost rivers and Birch Creek, which lose their aspirations in the aquifer of the Snake River Plain and reappear at Thousand Springs near the town of Buhl.

A subterranean water system, the aquifer encompasses about nine thousand square miles, making it among the largest in the world. It stretches from St. Anthony west to the Hagerman Valley. Though it appears on the surface to be bleak, volcanic slag, underneath it is highly porous, fractured basalt, where water percolates, accumulates, and moves generally east to west at a rate of perhaps ten feet a day. Perhaps. Only now are hydrologists developing the analytical tools, including computer models, to evaluate the aquifer. First estimates indicate that the water table between fifty and one hundred feet contains 100 million-acre-feet, and 10 percent of that passes through the aquifer each year, but a great deal is unknown. A larger knowledge of the workings of the watershed is urgently needed because over a million acres of south Idaho farm land draw upon it for irrigation.

The dynamics of the Snake Plain aquifer are only one aspect of the most complex question mark on the face of Idaho, a mark cut by the twists of the river itself. Water users in this region—and that means at least half the people in Idaho—are up against a bluff and there is no trail around. A brief history lesson may help to understand the problem in allocating the scarcest resource in the droughty West.

In 1894 Congress encouraged reclamation of desert lands by passing the Carey Act, which granted one million acres to each state able to irrigate those acres and settle individuals on 160-acre tracts within ten years. Since states could not afford to construct the irrigation projects themselves, they contracted with private enterprise. Companies obtained valid water rights, drew up construction plans, and applied to the state for development tracts. Once the state approved the plans, and water could be put on the land, it advertised that the tract was open to settlers. While the state had the exclusive power to regulate the water, the construction companies were given the privilege, as trustees, to sell water rights to the settlers in order to recover costs and a reasonable profit.

It was in this manner, under the persistent leadership of I. B. Perrine, that the Twin Falls South Side project (Magic Valley) reclaimed one-quarter of a million acres. Idaho was the second state to accept the Carey Act, and by 1930 over 600,000 acres were patented by settlers — more acreage in one project than in all the projects of the second-most successful state.

Low in organic matter, sagebrush lands are, nevertheless, inherently fertile and productive when irrigated, but they must be cropped in rotation with a soil builder like alfalfa. Gravity methods of irrigation, with lateral canals, rills, and flooding, were used on reclamation lands until after World War II, when aluminum pipe, sprinklers, and high-volume pumps became available. Irrigated land during the 1960s and 1970s increased by an average of 55,000 acres a year, most of it watered by sprinklers. Agribusiness has become the principal contributor to the economy of the state, and nearly three-fourths of Idaho's four million acres of irrigated farmland lie inside the Snake River drainage, upstream from Boise. As a result, the Snake has become a penstock-and-turbine river. Forty-three reservoirs have been built on the river and its tributaries to store irrigation water and produce the electricity for pumping it. Idaho Power Company built sixteen dams along the Snake, and, in the 1970s, recognizing a larger market for its power, urged farmers to divert the water and "make the desert-plateau bloom."

A dispute arose in 1977, however, when a group of Idaho Power's customers contended that the utility had allowed irrigation pumping from the river to diminish its hydroelectric power and thus required expensive coal-fired generators to replace the loss. Put another way, irrigating land to this extent reduces the river's flow and raises power rates even for the irrigators. The ratepayers filed a complaint, alleging Idaho Power was not defending its customers' water rights at Swan Falls Dam on the Snake, due south of Boise.

Swan Falls Dam was built in 1900 and acquired by Idaho Power in 1916. All of the surface and underground water of the Snake River drainage above Boise flows past this point. In 1929 the citizens of Idaho adopted a constitutional amendment stating that the legislature could make the upstream uses of water for households, farms, and factories superior to uses for power purposes. These "consumptive" priorities were spelled out in licenses for subsequent dams on the Snake built by Idaho Power. Until the suit was filed, everyone assumed that the subordination concept also applied to Swan Falls. Idaho Power counter-sued to determine the status of its water right. To the astonishment of many water law experts, the State Supreme Court ruled that the rights of Idaho Power to the historical flow of 8,400 cubic feet per second at Swan Falls are not subordinated. The decision, protecting low-cost energy, was remanded to the district court for determination.

The left-handed stinger in all of this is that existing flows in the Snake are now 6,000 cfs, and the legally established minimum flow, for environmental reasons, is 3,300 cfs. Were the district court to rule that Idaho Power owned all the remaining water in the river, any future use from ground or surface sources would have to come out of existing use, meaning there could be no agricultural growth.

In 1983 the legislature authorized the governor to enter into a contract with Idaho Power to recognize the water rights of about five thousand of the defendants. An agreement signed in October, 1984, by the governor, the state attorney general, and the chairman of Idaho Power involved at least a dozen changes in state laws and policies. In 1985 the governor signed six bills approved by the legislature, which set up the system to process claims and may permit new uses for 600 cfs from the Snake River. The arrangement calls for court adjudication, estimated to be a ten-year process, to determine who has what rights where. Adjudication on such a scale is larger than any other in the country's history and it may have implications for north Idaho's rivers as well.

"Of all issues confronting the lands of southern Idaho," says farm analyst Gale Chambers, "Swan Falls ... could be the most vital, emotional, and complex in the state's history." In a situation this complicated, where over half the diversions on the Snake system are not even measured, a comprehensive effort to understand the relationship between the aquifer and the river must be organized, and a balance struck by the legislature between uses, cost, and growth.

This is not a strictly Idaho predicament: it is a western one, as old as John Wesley Powell's 1878 *Report on the Lands of the Arid Region of the United States* — his long view has finally caught up with the future. The simple truth is that the Snake can no longer supply water to meet all the demands placed upon it at all times and at every location within its basin. Accommodating the needs or demands in one area with the applications or uses in another, the region will be forced to make decisions that will put their imprint on the heartland of Idaho for the next century.

Pocatello: Rails to Phosphoria

It is hot in Pocatello; the sun rides in a brazen sky, the air palpitates with fine dust, blowing in from the desert by way of the new roundhouses and out to the desert again by the brewery. But Pocatello minds neither dust nor heat, for is not this the dawn of her greatest day?

R. S. Baker
The Century Magazine
1903

Owing its existence to serendipity, Pocatello Junction was the point where the northern and western ambitions of the Union Pacific crossed. Track from the Utah Northern (Salt Lake-Butte) and the Oregon Short Line (Wyoming-Oregon) intersected on the Fort Hall Indian Reservation, and the Union Pacific decided this rendezvous site was suitable for its Idaho division point. Through a series of agreements, all properly sanctified by Congress, with the Shoshone-Bannock tribes, Pocatello became a townsite in the 1880s.

In 1898 the tribes—"a willing party to a losing bargain"—agreed to sell over 400,000 acres on the south end of their reservation to the federal government. Four years later the government announced that the area would be opened to settlement by using a land rush similar to Oklahoma's. On June 17, 1902, several thousand "sagebrush sooners" gathered at the borders of the former reserve. At noon each man or woman could run or ride for the land they coveted, post notice of possession, and then race to file their claim at the Land Office in Blackfoot, twenty-four miles north of Pocatello.

Journalist Ray Stannard Baker, who witnessed the "Day of the Run" wrote:

And so at last, at the end of interminable seconds, out blares the roundhouse whistle. They are off, neck and heel, driving home their spurs, doubled over their saddles, leaping sagebrush, all together, all confusion — riders, buggies, bicycles ... with monstrous clouds of dust rising behind, a great calvary charge, a sooner for every sage clump.

Once the land was taken up, the division point emerged as the principal town of southeastern Idaho; by 1920 its population of fifteen thousand qualified it under state law as a city of the first class. Pocatello was up to steam, if not up to full whistle. Now the city is the second largest in the state and is also the home of Idaho State University.

As Pocatello was a plexus of rail and then truck lines, large wholesale and manufacturing businesses were attracted to the area. During World War II, more than forty-five hundred railroad cars passed through the city's yard daily. Despite increased competition with other forms of transportation, at present Pocatello remains among the half-dozen busiest switching yards on the expanded Union Pacific system.

Proximity to the railroad was the primary consideration when James Kraft located a cheese processing plant in the city in 1920. The plant became Kraft Company's western distribution center (Alaska to California, Montana to Hawaii) and a major employer. Occupying a forty-acre tract at the north end of the city, it is equipped with sophisticated machinery designed by Kraft engineers to cut, package, and store millions of pounds of natural and processed cheese.

Four miles west of the city, Food Machinery Corporation operates the largest elemental phosphorous plant in the world alongside the J. R. Simplot factory, which manufactures solid and liquid fertilizers. Two million tons of phosphate are shipped by rail each year from the Gay mine on the nearby Shoshone-Bannock reservation to the FMC-Simplot complex. Tribal agreements negotiated by its business council in 1947 and 1960 provide for excavation of the deposits located on reservation land thirty miles northeast of Pocatello.

The Phosphoria Formation, deposited 230 million years ago by an inland sea connected to the ocean, extends from Rexburg south into Utah, but it is thickest and richest (about one hundred and fifty feet deep) in southeast Idaho. Estimated at one billion tons, these are the largest reserves in the nation, and provide about 15 percent of all United States production.

While the phosphate industry has become an important component of southeastern Idaho's economy, the mining itself may have long-term effects on wildlife habitat and water quality. Idaho's major phosphate processors provided $500,000 for a recent five-year study of possible effects and reclamation methods, in cooperation with the U.S. Department of Fish and Game, Caribou National Forest, and the Bureau of Land Management. Widespread commitment to the study is some indication of concern on the part of resource corporations.

North of Zion

The land cut, as it were, for them, a place
For them between the great divide and the sea.
There, he said in the voice of conscience, there
Is our home, or the hope of it.

C. F. Larson
"Homestead in Idaho"

Teton Dam, 300 feet high and 3,000 feet long, was completed in the spring of 1976, near the mouth of the engorged Teton River. By the first week of June, the reservoir behind the earth-filled structure was almost full. At noon on June 6 the dam split like a watermelon kicked by a mule.

"The sound was just like a roar," said a witness on the rim, "as if we were standing at the bottom of a waterfall. The powerhouse disintegrated as if it was made of cardboard. There was a beautiful grove of cottonwood trees, and they bowed over like matchsticks. There was a strange odor. I guess it was just the fresh dirt."

Moving at fifteen miles an hour, the deluge struck Sugar City and leveled its three hundred buildings. An hour and a half later it overwhelmed a thousand houses in Rexburg, then splayed down the valley to Idaho Falls, Shelley, and Blackfoot, and finally, three days after that, sated itself in the backwaters of American Falls Reservoir. In its wake it left thirty-five thousand acres of prime farm land ruined. Fremont, Madison, and Jefferson counties were the most severely damaged. The federal government, assuming responsibility for its "engineered flood" without admitting liability, paid $400 million in public and private damages. The final report on the adjustment program for the disaster area stated:

> Setting this disaster apart from others is the extent of self-help and voluntary assistance that have characterized the recovery effort. Organized by the Church of Jesus Christ of the Latter-day Saints (LDS), almost 15,000 volunteers were recruited in Idaho and neighboring states. About half the volunteers traveled into the area from out of state, some driving as much as 500 miles in a day, to bring support and help residents with clean-up work. All reports indicate this help provided a tremendous boost in morale to residents.

Approximately 80 percent of the persons living in the three overwhelmed counties are Mormons—members of the LDS Church. Labor, unity, and self-sufficiency are deeply embedded tenets of their faith, and the Teton flood offered a wide-scale demonstration of these traditions in practice. Ricks, a junior college in Rexburg operated by the Church, became the high ground for the relief effort and greatly mitigated the tremendous shock to members of the community who were awash in mud. Thousands were fed in the cafeteria; hundreds were housed in the dormitories. Estimates of the value of the labor provided by the Mormons exceeds $10 million.

The Saints first arrived in Idaho from the Salt Lake Valley at the direction of Brigham Young. In 1855 he ordered a band of twenty-seven missionaries to settle among the Shoshone and Bannock and "teach them the principles of citizenship." They founded the Lemhi mission on the Lemhi River, 330 miles northwest of Salt Lake. But because of grasshoppers and midsummer frosts, the settlement had difficulty establishing self-sustaining agriculture. After three years, and an attack by Indians, the site was abandoned and its people withdrew to the Salt Lake Basin.

As the differences between the federal government and Utah eased, the Mormon outreach to Idaho was renewed. In 1860 a "shepherded migration" of Mormon families entered the northern end of Cache Valley and, unaware that they had crossed the Utah border, established Franklin, Idaho's first Anglo-Saxon settlement and school. Within a few years, the parallel valleys of Bear Lake on the east and Malad on the west were also seeded with small communities whose agrarian labors—and they worked like honeybees in clover—were relieved by weddings, births, funerals, ward meetings, and Indian scares.

Until the U.S. Geologic Survey in 1872 clarified the territorial boundary, these immigrants mistakenly paid taxes to Utah and sent legislators to Salt Lake City. Even after the survey, Charles Rich, the founder of Paris, Idaho, continued to serve in the Utah legislature for a number of sessions, despite his Idaho residency, while his son repesented the same area in the Idaho legislature in Boise.

The Upper Snake River Valley was the last place in Idaho to be occupied by Mormon pioneers from Cache Valley. A major reason for the delay was Brigham Young's admonishment:

> The further we go north, the less good characteristics are connected with the valleys, except in articles of fish, water, and in some instances timber; and when the people are obliged to live in the north country that will be high time for them to go there.

At the present time, the Upper Snake River Valley is Idaho's most heavily populated Mormon region, with the greatest number of Latter-day Saints living in and around Idaho Falls.

Most of the areas settled in south Idaho by the Saints were dry as a wagon tongue, but the Mormons savvied irrigation—they dug the first ditches in the territory at Lemhi and Franklin. A kindred Mormon achievement, recognized as "one of the enduring contributions of the Church to the settlement of the West," was the development of a legal code, regulating the distribution of water, which was adopted by all the western states. The Mormons worked out a new law known as "prior appropriation:" unlike the eastern riparian code, stream water could be used for irrigation without returning an equal flow into the stream; early users therefore acquired permanent rights to water against all latecomers.

Predominantly Mormon areas of Idaho happen to overlay the state's most productive potato ground. Depending upon the year, potatoes and wheat take turns in being Idaho's number one crop. From 1950 to 1980 the state expanded its share of the United States market in potatoes from 12 percent to 27 percent. This growth was possible because sprinkler irrigation, better plant varieties, and better storage methods have been adopted at an increasing rate, and because Idaho potatoes are preferred by consumers—factors that compensate for low yields and an awkward shipping location in comparison to competing states.

When Brigham Young, the "Moses" of the Mormons died in 1877, there were thirty Mormon settlements in Idaho Territory. In the years that followed, because of their doctrines and their cooperative successes, Mormons encountered hostility similar to that which had plagued them in the East. In the 1880s Idaho legislation effectively prevented Church members from voting, holding public office, or serving on juries. Abandonment of plural marriage in 1890 was a concession by the Church; it altered the climate of criticism, and the glaciers of anti-Mormonism began to retreat. With a period of greater tolerance, Mormons in Idaho have realized political representation; a member of the Church has been elected to Congress from eastern Idaho in the last thirteen general elections.

Members of the LDS Church now comprise one-quarter of the state's population, and Mormon enterprises and endeavors have added a distinctive resiliency to the membrane of history stretching across southeastern Idaho.

IDAHO ENTIRE

Begin with a few trappers lost in fur.
Name a lake Henry, a town Fremont
a fort Hall, another place "The Woods."
Now very, very quietly say "gold"
and "silver"—just low enough
to wake one ear and change the world.

Jim Hepworth
"A Short History of Idaho"

Some Idahoans know that their state is home to Dean Oliver, three-time All Around Cowboy; Harmon Killebrew, elected to Baseball's Hall of Fame; and Jerry Kramer, pro football player and author. A few know that it is the birthplace of poet Ezra Pound; of novelist Marilynne Robinson; of actress Lana Turner; of sculptor Gutzon Borglum, who carved the faces on Mount Rushmore. And every Idahoan is vaguely aware that he lives with fewer doctors and more millionaires per capita than his fellow Americans. When Boise's newspaper, *The Idaho Statesman,* ran a contest asking for ways to tell a true Idahoan, the response ran to predictable rural and regional opinions. One Boisean said a native "can identify an alforja, a Jackson fork, a binder, a swamper, a jammer, a shay, a carp, and any source of natural fertilizer—blindfolded." According to a Meridian resident, a true Idahoan "is a person who doesn't plan a trip from southern Idaho to northern Idaho (or vice versa) because he knows he can't get there from here."

Yet it is apparent that the people of Idaho are increasingly urban, and that the state is not hyphenated in the way that it once was. We are leagued by rivers and roads; the water that shelves at Idaho Falls and Twin Falls is the same water that meets the barge leaving Lewiston; the trucks on U.S. 95 that call on Caldwell and Weiser take the same road to Moscow, Couer d'Alene, and Sandpoint. Transportation and communication have done much to consolidate the state. Additionally, we share a largely unspoiled landscape, which unites us in a common integument. We perceive inside that skin—an uncommon one in comparison to the rest of America.

Idaho is callow, last discovered and least altered of its neighbors. We have scars, of course: dredge dunes, the 1910 Fire, the clear-cut of the South Fork, Teton Dam; but we are fortunate enough to have had a few spokesmen—Ted Trueblood, Frank Church, Ernie Day, Cecil Andrus—who bought us time, the reprieve of youth. Their vision and exertion on behalf of an unscathed Idaho landscape are a reminder of what must yet be done and a reason for our regard.

Paradoxically, while Idahoans often disparage federal land ownership, only federal intervention, as historian Bernard DeVoto points out, was powerful enough to save western resources from total control and quick liquidation by absentee eastern owners. Federal intervention also preserved those resources from locally owned liquidation by the states. For that preservation the West, and Idaho in particular, is indebted. Permanent, sustained use of this wealth, whether water or timber, phosphate or solum, must be part of Idaho's blueprint.

In 1985 fewer than half of Idaho's residents were native-born. Writing about the state, author Robert Beatty said, "No one moves into Idaho, and no one ever will. Idaho moves into you." Presumably, newcomers recognize opportunities here that have been squandered elsewhere. Their efforts to preserve elements singularly Idahoan are as needed and valuable as any native's. And many natives have left the state, only to return. "To know the road ahead, ask those coming back."

Idaho's motto, visible at the uppermost edge of the state seal, reads, *Esto perpetua:* "May she endure forever." Only change is forever. Intelligent assessment of the problems inherent in change, and visionary solutions for them, are not inevitable; they are, however, all that will save our state identification. If we fail, the light on the mountains will fade like a morning dream—if we succeed it is a matter history will credit to our memory forever.

Right: Larches flare like candles among spruce in the Selkirk Range—autumn needles turn yellow and shed. This species is an important lumber tree for Idaho.

Left: Entangled reflections of young black cottonwoods readily explain the phrase "the shadowy St. Joe." A visitor boating upriver in 1907 remarked that the cottonwoods were so dense that their tops bridged the river. At that time the 120-mile-long waterway was one of the better trout fishing spots in the country — catches of nine-pound cutthroats were common. *Above:* The Kootenai Wildlife Refuge five miles west of Bonners Ferry was established in 1965, primarily for the more than two hundred species of waterfowl. The thirty-seven-foot dike along the Kootenai River was built in the mid-1920s to protect the lowlands.

Above: A snowy comforter over the Palouse Hills around Moscow protects, and eventually waters, sprouted winter wheat. The region's deep aeolian soil is highly fertile, and though most of it is now planted with grain, its natural grasses, especially blue-bunch wheat grass, once formed a dense turf. *Right:* Ski instructors cut loose on a three-mile run through Engelmann spruce and firs at Schweitzer Basin, eleven miles northwest of Sandpoint. High in the Selkirk Mountains, the ski area's annual snow depth is 120 inches.

Left: Known as "fish hawks," the osprey nesting on snags and pilings along Coeur d'Alene Lake are common summer residents. This population, one of the larger in the country, winters in the Gulf States and Central America. *Above:* The St. Joe, "river within a lake," has been an attraction for excursion boats since the turn of the century. Lakes on both sides of the river were essentially merged in 1906 by the backwaters of Post Falls Dam. *Overleaf:* Idaho's largest lake, Pend Oreille, as seen from a hillside above Hope, looking southwest at sunset.

Left: Biscuitroot grows alongside Highway 12 at the outskirts of Lewiston. Known to the Nez Perce and to Lewis and Clark as "cous," the roots of this plant were an important food source. They were gathered in large quantities to be eaten raw or ground into flour. The resulting cakes taste like stale biscuits. *Above:* Winter rape flowers appear at Southwick in May and bloom until temperatures rise or the soil dries. This winter annual from the mustard family is grown for birdseed or for processing as an industrial oil because its toxic products make it unfit for consumption by either humans or livestock.

Above: View of Lewiston at the confluence of the Clearwater (left) and Snake rivers from atop the old Lewiston Grade. Grain bins on the Clearwater are those at the Port of Lewiston. Headlands of the Palouse were an impediment to transportation between the "river city" and Moscow until the road (sixty-four curves in a two-thousand-foot climb) was opened in 1917. In 1979 a new highway was finished. *Right:* A fifty-year-old crib elevator ponders the sunset at Gifford. The bucket elevator leg lifts grain to the distributor head, where it is fed by gravity to bins.

Left: North Fork of the Clearwater before it is stilled by the Dworshak Reservoir. Draining the western flank of the Bitterroot Range, the North Fork cuts its way through the tertiary granites of the Bungalow Pluton, marked by vertical, high-angle jointing. The placid flow here reveals no sign that a ninety-mile reach downriver was the scene of boisterous high-water log drives every spring from 1930 to 1971. *Above:* Larkins Lake on the St. Joe-Clearwater divide is within the Mallard Larkins Pioneer Area.

Above: Winter wheat, planted in the fall, turns the hills of the Palouse virescent in spring. Galvanized steel storage tanks allow modern farmers to bypass commercial grain elevators and hold their grain in hope of a better market price. When this crop is sold, it will probably travel by truck to Lewiston, where it will be loaded on barges for Portland. *Right:* Florence Lake begets Old Man Creek in The Crags of the Selway-Bitterroot Wilderness. Sliding smoothly past a grove of subalpine fir, the stream begins its three thousand-foot plunge to the Lochsa River.

Left: Burnt Knob Lake viewed from Burnt Knob, 8,200 feet high, on the Nez Perce Trail Road. This is the longest road without services (115 miles) in the West. Subalpine fir, whitebark pine, and Engelmann spruce accept the first snow of winter. *Above:* Reflections in an ice collage on Florence Lake in the Selway-Bitterroot, the second-largest classified wilderness in the contiguous forty-eight states. Past glacial activity is evident in the higher regions. The area is drained primarily by the Selway River.

Above: A yearling bull moose, largest member of the deer family, forages at a wilderness lake in the Selway-Bitterroot. Moose can completely submerge and stay underwater well over a minute — adaptations that allow them to feed on aquatic plants pulled from lake bottoms. Mature animals eat fifty pounds of food a day. *Right:* Grand fir, Rocky Mountain maple, maidenhair fern, and thimbleberry fringe the South Fork of the Clearwater near Golden. In 1861 gold was discovered in this drainage, but it was 1929 before a highway reached the area.

Left: Lochsa River in the fall. The longest section (six miles) of Lewis and Clark's route that can still be identified is located on the headwaters of this stream. *Above:* The citron leaves of dogbane, *Apocynum,* along the South Fork of the Clearwater. The popular name is derived from the Greek word meaning "noxious to dogs." Animals avoided dogbane, but Indians used the fiber from the stems to make cords and nets. *Overleaf:* Cove Lakes in the Selway-Bitterroot Wilderness, where yearly snowfall may total 600 inches at some locations.

Above: Third-generation cowboy wrangles crossbred steers on the Heckman ranch, which covers several thousand acres at White Bird. *Right:* Falling from the Seven Devils Mountains to the Snake River, Granite Creek carves its way through the basalt bones of Hells Canyon. The field is the lower end of a homestead taken up in 1902 by Mart Hibbs and reacquired by the Forest Service in 1976. *Overleaf:* The Salmon River above Riggins moves steadily and tranquilly toward its confluence with the Snake, eighty-five miles away. In the late 1930s, a gold dredge operated profitably four miles downstream.

Left: An artistic legacy of the Nez Perce's ancestors, these petroglyphs are visible at Buffalo Eddy on the Snake River south of Lewiston. They were pecked with a small stone, probably within the last two thousand years, but their meaning is unknown. The site holds the second-largest collection of Inland Northwest-style rock art. *Above:* At White Bird Canyon, Highway 95 descends three thousand feet in just seven miles. In 1877 the canyon was a battlefield in the Nez Perce War: outnumbered warriors routed two companies of the United States Army, killing one-third of the command without loss to themselves.

Above: Snake River flows the color of pulverized jade at Pittsburg Landing. Twenty miles upstream in the heart of Hells Canyon, the river is more closely walled with basalt. *Right:* Confluence of the Main Salmon with the South Fork (top right). In the early 1960s, erosion caused by Forest Service timber sales destroyed the South Fork salmon runs—55% of the Columbia's summer chinook. Logging was ended in 1965 but has now been renewed and water quality is again deteriorating.

Left: No longer branded, log ends are spray-painted to indicate the sale from which they were cut: private, corporate, or Forest Service. Since truckers are paid by haul weight, every load is weighed at the mill and tagged with a paper slip. A percentage of the loads is scaled. Logs in this deck at the Boise Cascade mill in Cascade will be cut into one and two-inch boards. *Above:* Hermes mine near Stibnite was one of only two mercury deposits in the state. Discovered in 1902, little mercury was recovered until two rotary furnaces went into operation between 1942 and 1948 and produced 335 tons.

Above: Kayaker blows past an exploding pillow wave on the North Fork of the Payette, alongside State Highway 55. Compared to rafting, kayaking is a nascent sport in Idaho, but the wealth of unruly water lures increasing numbers of boaters. The fierce pitch of the Payette—seventeen hundred feet in fifteen miles—has also attracted the region's power company, which would like to divert the river through eleven miles of tunnels to develop 100,000 k.w. *Right:* Sixty-five percent of Idaho's land is open to outdoor public recreation. Near McCall, a nordic skier glides along a groomed track, one of many among the state's eighteen ski areas.

Left: Looking east across Payette Peninsula and Payette Lake toward McCall. An 830-acre state park and the summer camp for the University of Idaho School of Forestry occupy the point. For eighty years lakeside sawmills cut lumber from the surrounding forests of ponderosa pine and Douglas fir. *Above:* Inflatable kayaks, accompanied by licensed guides, test the Salmon River east of Riggins. *Overleaf:* Osborne ranch in New Meadows was settled in 1880. From 1884 to 1973 the Circle C, a few miles north, made the valley headquarters for a vast cattle operation.

Above: Sunrise on Tango Lake which lies in a cirque at the head of Loon Creek, a tributary of the Middle Fork. *Right:* Ponderosa pine, with cinnamon bark, overhangs the Salmon River Canyon at the top of the Dixie Road. Often called yellow pine or bull pine, the species prefers dry, well-drained sites. Though mature at one hundred and fifty years, if it does not fall victim to pine butterfly or western pine beetle, bull pine can live to be five hundred years old. Archaeological excavations in the canyon below indicate ancestors of the Nez Perce lived there eighty-five hundred years ago.

Left: An amateur river-runner positions his raft on the tongue of Rubber Rapid in Impassable Canyon, Middle Fork of the Salmon. One of the Middle Fork's twenty named rapids, Rubber is considered to have the largest waves in the river on high water. *Above:* Mixed conifer forest occupies a zone far above Panther Creek, named for the prevalence of mountain lions in its drainage. The nation's only cobalt mine is located on the headwaters of the stream, which flows into the Salmon River fifteen miles above the mouth of the Middle Fork.

Above: A commercial float trip camps at Survey Creek in Impassable Canyon of the Middle Fork. Since the first canoe trip in 1926, river traffic has grown to the point that several thousand persons are waterborne through the canyon by outfitters every summer. No roads extend into the 104-mile river corridor, and motorized boats are prohibited. *Right:* Batholithic granites, similar to those in the Sawtooths, are exposed in the Bighorn Crags, just east of the lower Middle Fork. The Crags are part of the River of No Return Wilderness.

Left: Basque musician in Ann Morrison Park. Arriving from four provinces in Spain and three in France, where they spoke their own language, Basques often worked as sheepherders before entering other occupations. By 1920, Boise Valley had become the nation's Basque center. Summer festivals with native music and dances are still held here. *Above:* With the invention of amalgamation-flotation concentrators in the 1930s, the Atlanta Mining District became Idaho's leading gold producer. The last mine closed in 1953, but numerous old houses remain.

Above: Rafting or tubing the Boise River through the greenbelt parks serves as the "great getaway" for 95,000 Boiseans each summer. Water flow on this part of the 190-mile river flow is regulated by Lucky Peak Dam. *Right:* Fruit, grapes, grain, sugar beets, and hay produce a variegated pattern in the Weiser Valley between Weiser and Payette. In the last twenty years, Idaho's farm population and farm workers declined by half. Yet in the same period, farm size doubled, productivity increased by 40%, and value per acre of farm land and buildings rose 500%. Of all farms in the state, 88% are family-owned.

Left: Local landmark, the Chateau-style Idanha Hotel on Main Street contrasts with the fourteen-story One Capital Center. The hotel was the first six-story building in the state, and contained Idaho's first elevator. In the 1970s, preservationists rescued it from an urban renewal project, while Capital Center was built on the first land purchased from the Boise Redevelopment Agency in a cooperative agreement leading to the hotel's restoration. *Above:* Capitol Dome and the Hall of Mirrors, which houses state offices. Reflective glass was chosen to save energy and to mirror the attractive surrounding buildings.

Above: Boise, "City of Trees," viewed from Camel's Back Park. *Right:* When finished in 1925, the Union Pacific depot at the southwest end of Capitol Boulevard was considered Idaho's finest example of Spanish Colonial architecture. *Overleaf:* Bogus Basin received its name when miners unearthed "fools' gold" on these mountains sixteen miles north of Boise. Six double chair lifts serve 2,000 acres and 1,800 vertical feet of skiing. Forty-three major runs are maintained, and night skiing is offered on three lifts.

Left: A thirty-three-mile portion of the Snake River Canyon has been set aside by the BLM as the Birds of Prey Natural Area for the preservation of nesting habitat for raptors. Basaltic cliffs, up to five hundred feet high, afford rearing sites for hawks, eagles, and falcons. Abundant ground squirrels on the desert back from the rim provide food. *Above:* Ferruginous hawks in Birds of Prey Area two days before leaving the nest. Parents use the nest for successive years. *Overleaf:* Country road and ranch southeast of Boise, only two miles off the Oregon Trail.

Left: Arrowleaf balsamroot is seen on dry hillsides throughout Idaho from April to July. Both flowers and leaves are the preferred spring food of bighorn sheep, and the plant withstands heavy grazing by livestock. *Above:* Appaloosa mare and foal near Boise. Though coat patterns vary with this breed, the snowflaked blanket is readily recognized. The horse was imported from China to Spain, then to Mexico, and then to Idaho, where the Nez Perce bred them. Admired for its endurance, the breed was first known as "a Palouse horse" for the Palouse River country.

Above: Willow weeps over early bale loader near Star. Ratchet chain, driven by axle gears, lifts bales from field to truck where they are stacked three-high. *Right:* Gold and silver lodes found in 1863 at Silver City gave the town the first telegraph service and newspaper in the Territory. A German-born carpenter crafted the details on John and Mary Stoddard's house, completed in 1895. The interior was richly furnished. Though "Silver" produced $40 million in precious metals, by the time the couple died in 1934, the site had become a ghost town.

Left: Jarbidge River Canyon in Owyhee County, looking south and up-canyon at Jarbidge Mountain in the Jarbidge Wilderness. Exposed Dorsey Creek Rhyolite, five hundred feet thick and 8 million years old, was extruded from volcanic fissures. Since the Jarbidge is a young river, one theory suggests water from a glacier on Jarbidge Mountain, rather than the present river, cut the one thousand-foot canyon within the last million years. *Above:* Little Jacks Creek Canyon, south of Grandview, serves as habitat for 125 rare California bighorn sheep.

Above: Indian paintbrush thrives among shadscale on the Owyhee Desert. A parasitic plant, paintbrush steals much of its food by penetrating the roots of other plants. Its pale leaves indicate low levels of the chlorophyll needed to make its own food. *Right:* Bruneau River, a tributary of the Snake south of Mountain Home, strops its way through a basalt canyon only a tew million years old. Each bench of basalt represents an eruption period of several flows from the same volcano, but the flows have yet to be named or dated.

Left: Two dunes cover six hundred acres and rise almost five hundred feet at Bruneau Dunes State Park. In 1952, C. J. Strike Dam raised the area's water table and created the lakelet at the base of the dunes. *Above:* Sage grouse near Oreana performs its April courtship display on the strutting ground, where polygamous mating occurs. Inflating air sacs on his neck, the bird releases a short, deep sound. Populations of this bird, whose diet is 70% sage, were reduced by overhunting and reclamation. *Overleaf:* Owyhee River at mouth of Battle Creek meanders through a 10 million-year-old rhyolite flow.

Above: Dow Dunning's homestead in Owyhee County served as the Wickahoney Post Office/Stage Station from 1895 to 1911, until an easier route was found from Mountain Home, by way of Elko, to the Nevada mines. *Right:* Waxy, April flowers of the nipple cactus, *Coryphanta missouriensis,* seen here south of Grandview, are a frequent sight on the Snake River Plain. Because half of the tiny plant is usually beneath desert pavement, often only the bloom is visible.

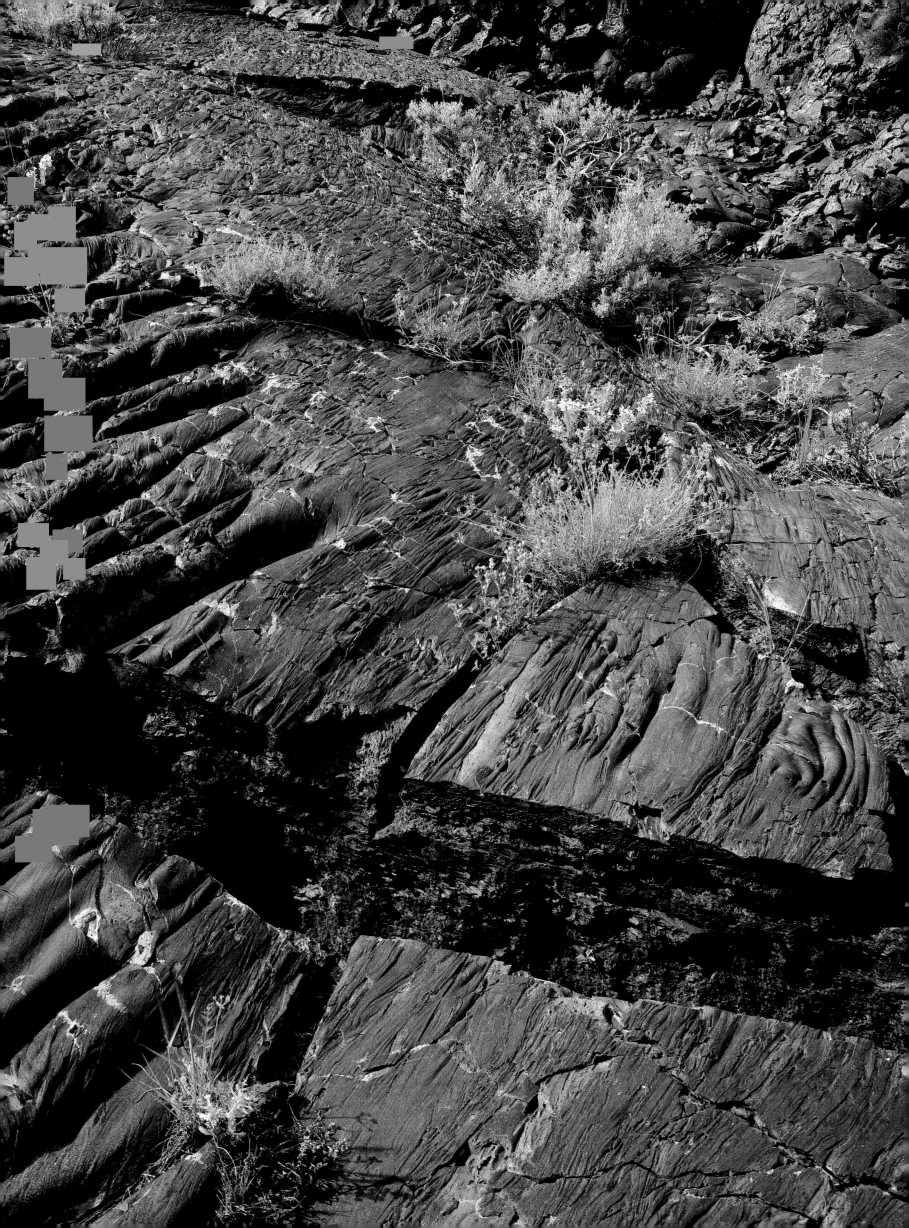

Left: Blue Dragon flow of pahoehoe lava at Craters of the Moon. Deep faults allowed the molten rock to ascend and flow easily beneath a stiffening but plastic crust, which cooled rapidly as it was dragged into viscous folds. This flow, dated from the carbonized roots of plants, is one of the youngest in the state. A thin, glassy film lends the lava surface its cobalt color — rare among the earth's lava flows. *Above:* Pillars left from a spatter cone after a lava flow transported them away from a vent to their present location.

Above: Dwarf purple monkeyflower, *Mimulus nanus,* prefers dry, open sageplains like those of the Owyhee Desert. In a year of poor rainfall all its effort goes into producing new seeds, and it puts forth only a single flower. *Right:* Once proposed as a national park, the 212-foot Shoshone Falls — the "Niagara of the West" — sunders the Snake River five miles from the city of Twin Falls. In 1907 the falls were first harnessed for electricity. Idaho Power Company acquired the generators in 1915 and constructed a diversion dam in 1927. By early summer, irrigation and hydropower siphon off most of the flow.

Left: Regionally famous balanced rock is poised sixteen miles southwest of Buhl. The cyclone-shaped stone is the remains of a column of cooled rhyolite which has weathered and spalled, leaving this forty-foot relic. *Above:* One of the "thousand springs" in Hagerman Valley releases water from the Snake River Plains aquifer into the Snake. Studies of percolation rates indicate that the water emerging here may have been underground for one hundred and fifty years. Along their upper face the springs are marred by a 650-foot concrete flume.

Above: Fort Hall is headquarters for the Shoshone-Bannock reservation: 1.8 million acres in 1869, 525,000 today — half tribally owned, half individually allotted. Linguistically, Shoshone and Bannocks are two distinct groups, but since both used the same region, which extended across southern Idaho, their cultures are treated as one. In August, the tribes' three thousand members hold their annual festival and rodeo. *Right:* Quaking aspens, like this grove on Indian Creek near the Wyoming border, flourish on high, cool sites with intense sunlight.

Left: Impressive limestone stalagmites are part of the half-mile tour through Minnetonka Cave, discovered in 1907 ten miles west of St. Charles by a grouse hunter. *Above:* When Idaho Falls was named in 1891, no falls existed at the site, but in 1911 the city built a diversion weir on the Snake for a power plant and substantiated the name. In 1978 residents approved a bond issue for three bulb-turbine power plants on the river — the only such municipally owned installations in the country. They provide 30% of the city's electricity. Across the Snake, the 165-foot pyramidal tower of the Latter-day Saints' temple indents the skyline.

Above: With thirty to thirty-five trains a day, the Pocatello railroad yard has more comings and goings than a tide table. It was the first automatic classification yard on the Union Pacific system and remains headquarters for the Idaho Division. Freight is largely potatoes, onions, sugar beets, frozen foods, and phosphate.
Right: Henry, first called Omega, was established in 1885 on the southeast side of Blackfoot Reservoir and was named for early settler Henry Schmidt. In 1965 its postal service moved to Soda Springs, but its tavern still serves.

OLY

OPEN

HENRY
CITY OFFICE.

7up
YOU LIKE IT... IT LIKES YOU

RASMUSSEN
Commissioner - 3rd Dist.

Left: Center-pivot sprinklers water a south Idaho potato field. Potatoes require high soil moisture before they are harvested in September or October. Sprinkler irrigation, begun in Idaho in the late 1940s, eliminated the need for level ground, produced a crop more uniform in quality, and reduced silt runoff from gravity irrigation. Idaho's growing conditions—warm days and cool nights—and its light soil produce a superior potato: the Idaho Russet Burbank, also called a Netted Gem. *Above:* Rancher bales hay beneath the west face of the Teton Range.

121

Above: Herder with dogs works his band of ewes off their bedground in Island Park. In Idaho only about eighty wool-growers still have bands (1,000 head) of sheep. *Right:* Showy, blue lupine is a wildflower whose genus name comes from the Latin ''lupus'' meaning wolf because it was once thought to deplete soil. In fact, it prefers poor soil. Several species are toxic to livestock. *Overleaf:* A site recommended for National Monument status by the National Park Service in 1972, City of Rocks outside Almo marries baroque geology of the Cassia batholith with several trails important to American emigration.

Left: Unnamed peak and pond in the Lost River Range, Challis National Forest. *Above:* A pair of mule deer spook from their beds on a mountainside in central Idaho. Large ears are responsible for the name. White-tail deer, a separate species, are more common in the northern part of the state and range as far south as the Salmon River. Antlers begin to grow in May, when increased daylight stimulates the buck's pituitary gland to release the hormone controlling antler growth. Velvet, as the network of veins is called, is a vascular skin that nourishes the antler from outside. When the antlers are grown, bucks can rid themselves of velvet in a day.

Above: Limber pine, *Pinus flexilis,* grows at elevations as high as 11,000 feet. With twigs so flexible that they can be tied in a knot without breaking, the species favors high, wind-swept ridges. A specimen growing in the Sawtooths was found to be 1,700 years old. *Right:* Charcoal kilns in Birch Creek Valley fueled the smelter for the Viola lead mine. It took a week to load the thirty-five cords of wood, burn it, and unload eight tons of charcoal from each kiln. Built in 1886, the kilns operated for six years. Of the original sixteen, only four survive.

Left: South end of the Lost River Range, looking south to Big Southern Butte. Paleozoic sediments (260-360 million years old) deposited in an inland sea have been tilted by Basin and Range faulting. Big Southern Butte, 7,576 feet high and a National Natural Landmark, is a separate geological feature: a volcanic, rhyolitic dome 300,000 years old. *Above:* Mount Borah in the Lost River Range. The state's highest point at 12,662 feet, it was named for William Borah, Idaho Senator from 1907 until his death in 1940.

Above: Rocky Mountain bighorn, *Ovis canadensis,* surveys his surroundings from a perch in the Lost River Range. Exceptional vision allows this healthy 5½ year-old ram to detect hand movements at a distance of one mile. *Right:* On October 28, 1983, Borah Peak earthquake, magnitude 7.3, struck sparsely settled central Idaho causing two deaths and $12.5 million in damage. Looking southeast from the vicinity of Willow Creek Summit toward the western boundary of the Lost River Range, one can see an eight-foot throw along some sections of the new scarp.

Left: Rocky Mountain iris, sometimes called western blue flag, indicates water close to the ground surface. It has no forage value for game or livestock. *Above:* Bull rider in jeopardy at the Mackay rodeo—billed as "Idaho's Wildest." *Overleaf:* Looking up Mammoth Canyon from Birch Creek Valley, Paleozoic sediments are visible along the east face of the Lemhi Range. On the left, Bell Mountain, 11,612 feet high, is named for Robert Bell, a former state mine inspector. A Natural Area just west of the peak is preserved as a botanical study area by the Forest Service.

Above: Great horned owl, one of fifteen species known to occur in the state, was first recorded in Idaho by the Lewis and Clark Expedition at Kamiah. Ear tufts were called "horns," but the ears are actually under the feathers of the skull, behind the face, and help more than eyes in the detection of prey. The owl can kill porcupines, skunks, and geese but prefers a diet of small rodents, such as mice. *Right:* Grouse Creek on the east side of the Lost River Range is absorbed by valley sediments before it ever reaches the Pahsimeroi River.

Left: Black cottonwoods, known to the Indians as "the tree that talks to itself," on the Salmon River between Challis and Salmon. *Above:* Pair of Rocky Mountain bighorn rams in central Idaho. Males generally spend the summer in subalpine areas and move down to more sheltered sites for the winter. Annual rings on the horns of the rams indicate their age. At five years of age they will have grown two-thirds of their overall length. Massive horns make good fighting weapons: during the rut, rams lunge at each other at combined speeds of twenty miles per hour and the resounding clash may be heard a mile away.

Above: Cowboy near Challis moves his Black Angus toward fall roundup. While sales of cattle and calves rank first in cash receipts among agricultural commodities in Idaho, public lands produce enough forage for only 4% of the nation's cattle — most are raised in feedlots. *Right:* An introduced, troublesome weed, Foxtail barley, sometimes called tickle grass, grows in irrigated meadows near Challis. Tolerant of alkalai, the tufted perennial thrives in slightly disturbed areas and causes problems for livestock in the form of sore eyes and mouths.

Left: Boulder Mountains, 11,000 feet in elevation, are flanked with aspen and Douglas fir near Galena Summit. *Above:* Widely distributed throughout Idaho, elk are most numerous in roadless timbered areas. Snow depth has profound effects on habitat use: twelve inches can force the animals to shift from grass to shrubs. Elk are known to respond to low barometric pressure and to gather on south-facing slopes in winter. This herd feeds on Fairfield's Camas Prairie, before the bulls shed their antlers in March or April.

Above: White Cloud Peaks, Merriam (left) and Castle, reflected in an alpine pond. Merriam Peak was named for Dr. John Merriam, founder and first president of the Greater Sawtooth Preservation Council. Rocks nearly white with metamorphic silicates suggested the name for the White Clouds themselves. *Right:* Seep-spring monkeyflower blooms from July to September along Broad Canyon Creek at the south end of Copper Basin. This member of the figwort family only requires a wet spot to grow at sea level or on a mountain slope.

Left: Discovery between 1875 and 1879 of the Charles Dickens and General Custer gold mines resulted in a rush to establish Bonanza City and Custer on Yankee Fork, a tributary of the upper Salmon River. Challis became the supply center. Running thirty stamps for a decade, the General Custer mill produced $8 million. Much of Bonanza was destroyed by fire in 1897. Fourteen years later, with the closure of the Sunbeam mine, Custer's clock stopped. *Above:* Custer's old schoolhouse now contains the McGown museum, staffed by the Forest Service during the summer.

Above: Alpine skier challenges moguls on Sun Valley's Mount Baldy, which has thirty-four hundred feet of vertical drop. Demanding slopes are groomed daily to attract the finest skiers in the world. *Right:* Mount Regan, 10,190 feet, nurtures Sawtooth Lake. *Overleaf:* Dawn breaks on the ragged blade of the Sawtooth Range, southwest of Little Redfish Lake. The mountains are part of a 16,000-acre wilderness within the 754,000-acre Sawtooth National Recreation Area, which was established in 1972. Forty-two of the peaks exceed ten thousand feet.

Above: Sun Valley condominiums huddle beneath 9,360-foot Bald Mountain. When the Janss family of California purchased Sun Valley from Union Pacific in 1964, Baldy served about one thousand skiers a day. Development of the Warm Springs side of the mountain, along with forty-three runs and fourteen chair lifts, allows the world-renowned mountain to handle fifteen thousand skiers an hour.
Right: Sunset near Hill City, northeast of Mountain Home. This area was discovered by Donald Mackenzie's fur trade party in 1820 and was used by emigrant wagons in 1852. The route was named Goodale's Cutoff after 1862, when it became a popular shortcut on the Oregon Trail from Fort Hall to Boise.

Left: White-rayed mule's ears, *Wyethia helianthoides,* flower in May and June in dense patches below the Boulder Mountains. Heads usually appear turned toward the sun. Deer and elk graze the young leaves. *Above:* Fly fishermen catch and release rainbow trout on Silver Creek Preserve, part of The Nature Conservancy management area just south of Bellevue. Beginning in 1976, Preserve acreage was purchased in an effort to save the spring-creek ecosystem while allowing farming, hunting, and fishing on the fifteen hundred acres.

Above: Resplendent aspens encircle a stand of somber Douglas fir on a slope near Sun Valley. Though quaking aspen seeds are wind-distributed, most new trees sprout from existing, extended roots. Logged for pulpwood, an aspen forest can reproduce itself in fifty years. *Right:* Scissored silhouette of Castle Rock juts several hundred feet above the East Fork of the Big Lost River in Copper Basin. Originally a solid mantle resulting from the Challis Volcanics 45 to 50 million years ago, the spire has eroded into bewitching hoodoos.